Where We Sported and Played

To Mary

In fond memory of happy days in Corfu.

Teddy 16.6.'91.

WHERE WE SPORTED AND PLAYED

Confessions of a Cork Boy

Teddy Delaney

THE MERCIER PRESS

The Mercier Press,
4 Bridge Street, Cork
24 Lower Abbey Street, Dublin 1

First published, 1991

ISBN 0 85342 964 2

ACKNOWLEDGEMENTS

*The author would like to thank Cork Examiner Publications Ltd., and
the* Irish Messenger *for permission to quote from their material.*

*He would also like to point out that the names of characters in
this book do not refer to any living person or persons and any
resemblances to such is purely coincidental.*

Printed in Ireland by Colour Books Ltd.

CONTENTS

In Memory of my Father
LEO DELANEY, 1922–1988
and my mother
BREDA OWENS, 1925–1988

1

HOME

In the *History of Cork* Cusack could be said to have amended the proverbial 'there's no place like home' to 'there's no place like Cork' thus:

> *Cork is the third city in the kingdom in regard to population, wealth and commerce, and may lay claim to be the first for the intelligence, enterprise and unbounded generosity of its merchant princes, and its warm-hearted and cultivated people. Nowhere, even in charitable Ireland, is charity more abundantly and ungrudgingly given, and the names of Cork men who have taken the highest place in literature are so numerous that, after some consideration, we have omitted mention of individual names, as a separate volume would be required to record their successful careers.* (History of Cork, M.F. Cusack, 1875)

And strange as it may seem, over 100 years later, Cork people still believe that crap about themselves. My two maternal uncles, Danny and Denis, were staunch custodians of this belief and whenever I'd dare question them would ream off a whole load of facts to prove their case: that by the year 1760 Cork was one of the most important towns of Europe with a population of 60,000, while Liverpool and Birmingham with only 30,000 each and Glasgow with 26,000, were miles behind. We had a choice of our own stout in Murphy's and Beamish's and weren't dependent on the Dublin crowd at St James' Gate. Our Buttermarket exported its produce all around the globe. We had our own special game of bowling, and wasn't Patrick's Street the finest street in Europe only for the bend in it? We had Dunlops and Fords where you could eat your dinner off the floor.

Sure 'twas no wonder that all the famous people came to Cork first: Spenser who wrote *The Faerie Queen* in Bandon, Walter Raleigh who brought tobacco and potatoes to Youghal, Thackeray and Charlotte Brontë. Of course we had our own great writers too: Daniel Corkery who wrote about the county, Frank O'Connor who wrote about the city, and Fr Prout who wrote *The Bells of Shandon* with rhymes the like of which were never heard in the English language before, and *The Groves of Blarney* not just in English but in other languages as well — including Latin, Greek, French and Italian, which Garibaldi sang in the spring of 1859 when camping in the woods near Lake Como. We had the painter Barry and the scientist Boyle and the great patriots, the Sheares brothers, Tomás MacCurtain and Terence MacSwiney.

Then, carried away completely, Denis would burst into a patriotic verse:

> *The war was over,*
> *Our men were sober*
> *They were not down-hearted,*
> *For the car was there.*
> *They were four of the bravest,*
> *Of the bold Sinn-Féiners*
> *That rescued McNellis,*
> *From Cork County Jail.*

My Grandmother would interject with 'and what about the great churchmen, Bishop Delaney, Dean Sexton and Fr O'Callaghan and the great nuns, Nano Nagle and Mary Aikenhead, who founded the Presentation Order and the Irish Sisters of Charity? Then Danny, bursting with pious pride, would solemnly deliver *The Beautiful City of St Finbar:*

Where We Sported and Played

I have travelled long and have travelled far,
And have seen great cities beyond the sea;
But none of them all seemed so fair to me
As the beautiful city of St Finbar.

Many rivers are greater and grander far,
Yet none do I love like the gentle Lee:
Whose murmuring tide chants soft melody
As it glides through the city of Saint Finbar.

Right splendid's the home of the Russian Czar,
Gay Paris looks bright on the banks of the Seine,
Old Rome by the Tiber is glorious, I ween:
But fairer the city of Saint Finbar.

Were I to choose where my life should be spent,
I'd build my cottage or pitch my tent,
And happily live, and die content
In the beautiful city of Saint Finbar.

'True for ye, boy,' Denis would add, 'and haven't we our own newspapers too, *The Examiner* in the morning, for the well-to-do, and *The Echo* in the evening for the working-class,' and he'd burst into song again. This always irritated my grandmother and she'd interrupt him with 'will ye shut up out a dat and sing something decent from the Opera House like *The Bohemian Girl* or *Maritana*.'

That was the *craic* in my mother's home place in Cook's Lane, off Shandon Street, on Saturday evenings in the early 1950s. I remember it better by its food smells: those of slaughter houses and bakeries and almost every smell in between. Mother believed it was the only place you could buy real fresh wholesome food: backbone and bodice, skirts and kidneys, tripe and drisheen, *crúibíns* and trotters and the tail-end of corned beef from Paddy Twomey's for the Sunday dinner. Her paternal aunts, Maggie and Molly, who

9

sold toffee-apples, always lit a tar barrel to welcome De Valera to Cork, around which they gathered, torches in hand, to sing *Legion of the Rearguard,* and were remembered for battering an actor off the stage of the Opera House when he had the cheek to come and his heyday long past.

Mother was six, the oldest of four, when her father, Taedy Owens, died. He fought on the American side in the First World War, and got a job in Ford's when he came home in 1922. He got sick and depressed in 1931. When my grandmother and mother came from town on 30 July they had to force the door open and found him dead. For the next fifty-six years they protected each other and spoke about everything but that traumatic shock. My grandmother died of old age in 1986. My mother hung on for another two years and then followed her parents.

Grandparents spoil their grandchildren. My grandmother was different. She put the fear of God in us. Tragically widowed at twenty-eight she had to be tough and would have gone to pieces if she showed emotion. Before she married my grandfather she had been engaged to Joe Murphy, but he died after seventy-six days hunger-strike in Cork Jail in November 1920. Fate dealt her a cruel hand but two things sustained her: her faith and her pedigree. She said the Rosary and made the Stations of the Cross every day. Her maiden name was O'Leary and she was as proud and bold as Art himself. (The fearless Irish outlaw, subject of the famous lament by his wife Eibhlín Dhubh Ní Chonaill, shot dead near Macroom on 4 May 1773 by the bodyguard of the High Sheriff, Abraham Morris.) Her mother was not just an O'Sullivan, but an O'Sullivan Beare. Grandmother had two cleaning jobs, one early in the morning in Shaw's Mills, the other in the afternoon in a big house in Blackrock. She retired when she was seventy. On festive occasions she took a drink and all the pent-up emotion and anger flowed. She was mad at everyone: the government, the clergy, my father's people, us. We all took my mother's advice and stayed out of her way except for my sister Mai, who frowned on my grandmother's behaviour. If she was mad at no one in particular before this she'd let Mai have it now: 'get out of my sight, ye brazen whip, ye saucy article, ye good for nothing Wakefield's melt, or I won't be responsible for what I'll do to ye!'

Although drink and its evils horrified my mother she often seemed happy at my grandmother's indulgence. She never had any such relief herself and would have made a good Carmelite nun. She was as happy as a Carmelite nun in her life of service and sacrifice and suffering. She was patient and proud of all of us and deeply saddened when, stuffed with sweets, we wouldn't eat our Christmas dinner. She'd remind us of Christmas 1931, the year her father died, of her expectation and excitement hanging up her Christmas stocking, and of her devastation in the morning to find that there was nothing in it. She was fanatically committed to ensuring that none of us would suffer the same deprivation and she insulated us with prayer and kindness. When lighting the candle on New Year's Eve she thanked God for the year past and prayed the next would be as good. Then she would give us older ones a loaf of bread and tell us to beat the inside of the front door with it, repeating the following refrain three times as we did so:

Goodbye old year
Welcome new year
Beat out hunger
Bring in plenty.

When I was two and a half years old we moved from Shandon Street to near my father's place on the Lower Road. 'Twas like moving from the Fall's Road to the Shankill. My grandfather Jim Delaney was from Laois, or Queen's County as my father's mother preferred to call it.

Where We Sported and Played

He came to Cork with the railway and married Alice Wakefield from Mallow, who was six years his senior. Other than that I know nothing about either of their backgrounds or families apart from rumours of rich relations in America and Australia, and that my grandmother's people were Protestant. My father was the oldest of four and the only one to remain at home. The other three went to England as soon as they could, as though to escape from the twilight zone in which Jim and Alice Delaney lived.

In her imagination we still lived in the glory days of the empire. She thought the Irish Free State a wash-out and the Republic a barbarity. To her, Cobh was always Queenstown and MacCurtain Street, King's Street. She considered herself, and may well have been, aristocracy on the way down, and was extremely proud of her hallstand with its brass gong, her ornamental plant pots and her picture of Queen Victoria. She hadn't a clue who Thackeray was but, when someone pointed out to her a book in the CIE Dormitory building in Water Street in which he bestowed lavish praise on her side of the city, she delighted in reading the following to me:

> We arrived at the beautiful wooded village of Glanmire, with its mills and steeples and streams, and neat school houses and pleasant country residences. This brings us down upon the superb stream which leads from the sea to Cork. The view for three miles on both sides is magnificently beautiful. Fine gardens and parks and villages cover the shore on each bank: the river is full of brisk craft moving to the city or out to sea; and the city finely ends the view rising upon two hills on either side of the stream. I do not know a town to which is an entrance more beautiful, commodious and stately. Passing by numberless handsome lodges and, nearer the city, many terraces in neat order, the road conducts us near a

12

large tract of some hundred acres which have been reclaimed from the sea and are destined to form a park and pleasure-ground for the citizens of Cork. In the river and up to the bridge some hundreds of ships were lying, and a fleet of steamboats opposite the handsome house of the St George Steam Packet Company (Irish Sketch Book).

She contrasted this praise with the lambasting Alexander the Coppersmith gave my mother's home place, which she found in another book in the library:

Here I will conclude Mallow Lane, i.e. Shandon Street, that nursery of villainy, which should be suffered to continue no longer, but presented, and removed as a nuisance, for when Honesty was sick in Glenflesk, she crawled to Mallow Lane to dye, and Maitre Coquin *assured me, that she gave her last groan amongst the butter buyers.*

And she'd round the lot off by comparing the common place-names on my mother's side, Cook's Lane, Knapp's Square, Clancytan and Cockpit Lane with the elegant and exotic Tivoli, Montenotte, Myrtle Hill and the Oriental.

My grandfather was a quiet gentleman who smoked Woodbines which he always topped to prolong his daily ration of ten. They were caretakers at the Railway Dormitory looking after the Dublin train crews at Water Street, had a free house, light and coal and were very independent. They mixed very little and on Sunday mornings took the 11.00 bus to town for 11.15 mass in St Augustines. My father and I went with them for years. We were never on time and only managed to get inside the side door on Washington Street. Just as well, for I found the place frightening, like the ante-chamber of the Inferno. It was dark and gloomy and smelling of candle grease and had a gruesomely realistic crucifixion scene with life-size characters dripping blood and the biggest nails I ever saw. Through the door, over the altar, a reproduction Guido Reni depicted a scene of utter desolation, while to the left hung a picture of St Patrick triumphantly casting the snakes out of Ireland. The sermon was always valley of tears stuff, full of chastisement and retribution. Then a battalion of lay volunteers with bags attached to long sticks moved through the crowd and everyone had to pay. I thought that they would have it in for me because I never had any money, and I imagined them raking the ashes of hell with their long sticks to receive my sinful soul.

My father was the last of the great Lower Road fishermen. He had his own boat and nets and never had a licence. He served his apprenticeship with Looney John from the time he was twelve and often had the coal house full of salmon in the morning, having poached all night under the noses of the bailiffs. I learned a lot about boats and fishing from him: about the properties of hard and soft woods: the pliability of larch and the resistance of oak; the buoyancy of cork and the weight and malleability of lead; how to caulk and red-lead taper and splice a rope.

If my father was challenged by the law he'd reply that it was his birthright to fish the Lee and that was that. He wouldn't have been able to substantiate his claim, but if told that this right was based on a grant under the Acts of Settlement and Explanation made to Richard and Henry Tickborne and Major John Griffiths on 17 November 1668 of *inter alia* 'Glanmire weare', would have replied, 'There ye are now. Sure I know that, boy!'

He was a man of endless patience and spent a lot of time putting boats into bottles. He also considered himself a bit of a poet and, after an hour or two musing within himself, would produce the likes of:

Where We Sported and Played

Teddy and Alice
Saw a film in the Palace.
John and Mai were playing in the hay.
Ronnie and Anne ate marzipan.

At other times he imagined he was Mario Lanza and would burst into a full-throated rendition of:

Overhead the moon is b-e-a-m-i-n-g,
White as blossoms on the bough.
Nothing is heard but the song of a bird
Filling all the air with d-r-e-a-m-i-n-g.

Fishing terminology peppered his speech. Everything with him was either bow or stern, forrad or aft. Life itself was a matter of gaffs, strauch-hauling and feathering your oar. He had other words too that don't appear in any dictionary of slang: corner-boys he always referred to as 'pocket-billiard players'; after dinner he went down the 'flags' to talk to the 'lads'. The 'lads' were all at least as old as himself, and it was so long since concrete had replaced the flagstones that nobody could remember.

He convinced us that the Lower Road was the centre of the world. We played in 'The Quarry', or 'The Strand'. The ESB transformer station at the top of the lane was the 'Shannon Scheme', the local CIE snooker hall, 'The Dive'. As I grew older I found it disturbing to learn that the Lower Road was not the Platonic model God used to design everywhere else; 'The Strand', was only a strand, 'The Quarry', a quarry; the 'Shannon Scheme', was really at Ardnacrusha in Co. Limerick and, when I finally learned that 'dive' was an American slang word for a sleasy joint of ill-repute where people misspent their youth, I was devastated. The Lower Road was not the world after all and my disillusionment grew with me. The magic died and the milkman, the bus driver and the shop-keeper in the stage one primary school reader were no longer the kind, smiling, friendly illustrations of the book.

Unlike my father, my mother never used slang, but had a number of expressions that perplexed me. She was a master of charitable understatement: 'she's a very big girl, God bless her ', she'd say about a big fat lump of a woman, or 'she's very plain, God bless her ', about an ugly hag. Of my father's penchant for cheap ornamentation (he gilded everything and hung shillelaghs all over the place), she'd say: 'he's all fal-dolls' and, on the necessity for discretion about family matters out of doors, she told us not to be 'filling their mouths'. I never once heard her utter a vulgar word, and woe betide any of us who did. She never slapped any of us, except me, on one occasion.

I remember it as the first major *faux pas* in my life. I was eleven years old and spending a lot of time looking over my shoulder lest my mother catch me indulging in my lately acquired street ways and words. I had a premonition that it was only a matter of time before I'd make a slip-up. My biggest fear was that a whole litany of dirty words would come out while I slept, words like 'bitch','bollocks', 'prick', and I could do nothing about it. In actual fact it happened quite differently. It was Saturday night. The word of the week was 'hole', and I was so conscious of its dirty value that I handled it rather nervously. My mother was on her knees polishing the shoes for mass next morning. We had all just been bathed and I was standing on a chair near the fire. 'Did any of ye see the polish brush?' my mother asked. The devil within me answered "tis up me hole'. My mouth stayed open in a broad O of astonishment. My mother was thunderstruck. Then she rose to her feet mechanically, made a bee-line for me and leathered and flaked me across the back of the legs. She sent me straight to bed without supper and I was sorry for having shocked her so, but somewhat relieved that I could go about my business now with a clear conscience. I had paid for my transgression and so there was no need to feel guilty any more.

The worst part of my punishment was that I missed the best part of the Saturday night ritual, the special supper of a cup of raza and one of Sunday's queen cakes, and I felt awfully lonely as I lay in bed listening to the pleasant sounds from the kitchen as my mother jigged the baby, Anne, up and down on her knee and led them through all our favourite songs and poems:

There was a little man
and he had a little gun
and his bullets were made
out of lead, lead, lead,
and he went to the brook
and he shot a little duck
down, down, down, dead.
And he brought it home
To his old wife Joan
and he said
Put down a big, big big fire
for to roast the little duck
that was swimming in the brook
and tomorrow I'll bring you
a big, fat hen.

Then they all broke into a chorus of:

Clap handies, clap handies
till Daddy comes home.
He has cakes in his pocket
for An-ne alone.

and

17

Where We Sported and Played

We'll take Anne walking
and we'll take her up the Dyke.
We'll take Anne walking
and we'll dress her all in white.
She is the doll in Cash's window;
she is a doll and a dill doll day.

Then I began to cry and cried myself to sleep.

Some of my mother's songs I didn't like at all.

My mama told me
if I was goodie
that she would buy me
a rubber dolly.

was one that perplexed me for years. As I understood it, a doll was a girl's toy, but a 'rubber dolly', was a shoe and 'twas no good if your mother only bought you one. I had the same difficulty with the lines:

see the tender lamb appear
promised from eternal year

in the Christmas hymn *See amid the Winter Snow*. I understood the lamb appeared 'from his prom', thinking it some kind of sheepfold. In the same way it took me years to figure out the road sign which read *cul de sac*. I knew that *cúl an tí* meant behind the house but *cul de sac* had me flummoxed.

On Sunday night, when Ronnie and Anne were gone to bed my mother sat Alice, Mai, John and myself down around the fire and read us stories from *The Irish Messenger*. Every word of them was true and better than *The Beezer* or *Bunty* any day of the week. There were dramatic last confession stories from the First World War like:

Where We Sported and Played

'Dublin and Proud of It (a True Story)', which opened with a bigger bang than anything in *The Victor*.

> *S-S-S-SEP! Cr-r-e-r--rump!! Whee-e-e-iou hrumph!!!*
> *Bullets snapped and whined; shells screamed*
> *overhead; the air swayed in the frightful tempest of*
> *rushing metal; the ground reeled under the tremendous*
> *thuds that smote it. The young officer hugged more*
> *closely the side of the shell-hole in which he*
> *crouched. 'My God,' he groaned, 'this is awful! Will it*
> *ever stop?' Suddenly there was a roaring whirlwind,*
> *a deafening crash, and the earth seemed to throw*
> *itself at the skies as a huge shell tore a cavern for*
> *itself in the ground close by, and disappeared in a*
> *cloud of flame and smoke. 'That's hot stuff!' said a*
> *cheery voice. The young officer looked and saw an*
> *Army Chaplain smiling down at him from the edge of*
> *the shell-hole.*

The letters of thanksgiving were real *Alice in Wonderland* stuff. There were miraculous escapes:

> *Co Wicklow. Dear Rev Father –A few nights ago when*
> *going to bed I was very tired and yet I decided to read*
> *a little before going to sleep. I said my prayers and left*
> *my beads beside me and then I took up the Messenger*
> *and read a story. All this time the candle was beside*
> *me in the bed and not on the table beside the bed. This*
> *was a dreadful thing to do but it fulfilled its own*
> *purpose. I lay with my head exactly on level with the*
> *candle and had not read for very long when I fell*
> *asleep. At 7.30 a.m. I awoke, and found my beads and*
> *the Messenger beside me, and also the empty candle-*
> *stick. (I had put in a new candle the night before.) I*
> *looked about for the candle thinking it had rolled*
> *under the bed clothes, but no! it had burnt out com-*

pletely as well as some of the brown paper at the end of it. When I realised what had happened – that I had slept all night with a lighted candle beside my head, with an eiderdown etc. which could so easily have caught fire and either burned me to death or else burned my hair and face badly – you can imagine my feelings. I got up at once and went to Mass and Holy Communion to thank the dear Sacred Heart for His care of me even when I did not ask Him. I shall keep that Messenger always as a memento – A Lover of the Sacred Heart.

Lucky breaks for Irish Catholic exiles across the Irish Sea:

London. Dear Rev Father – Please publish my thanksgiving. 'Ask and you shall receive'. This message has been my comfort and consolation. Since I left Ireland as a young and friendless girl I have lived amidst London's guilt and temptation, but constant prayer has been my anchorage. I wish I could name all the gifts and graces the Sacred Heart has poured on me in one long stream. My work is difficult and though I had little training for it I had infinitely more success than highly qualified associates. I consecrate each day to the Sacred Heart as I go to work and at night return thanks. On three occasions I had displays and our organisers who know the work intimately were wonder-struck at the success of them, and the spectators were amazed. I prayed for a good husband and have been granted that favour and I am now confidently praying for a Catholic home – London-Irish.

Remarkable sporting success:

Ireland. Dear Rev Father – Some time ago I was elected captain of the local hurling team. I made a promise to the Sacred Heart that if my team won the Championship I would publish a thanksgiving in the Messenger. *Strange to relate, when everything was going against us on the field I placed my trust in the Sacred Heart and repeated the ejaculation, 'Sacred Heart of Jesus I place all my trust in Thee', and to the surprise of all we won on the whistle.*

Hoping you will find space to show your readers what the Sacred Heart can do if you only trust in Him – A Fond Lover of the Sacred Heart.

Then there were the fascinating lists of thanksgivings classified under various headings. Health had specifics like:

Baby boy recovers from kick of horse.
Little girl cured of St Vitus dance.
Cure of injured knees after seven years suffering.
Recovery of health after blood poisoning without loss of finger.
No ill-effects after being bitten by a mad dog.
Preserved from serious injury when attacked by a lunatic.

The range was from the major:

Miraculous escape of brother from instantaneous death in terrible accident.
Escape from death on three occasions.

to the minor:

Ugly wart removed from neck.
Saved from effects of sting on tongue.

Bicycles featured prominently:

21

Where We Sported and Played

> *Escape from serious accident when bicycle skidded in front of motor car.*
> *Marvellous escape from injury when bicycle brakes refused to work.*

Sporting, recreational and cultural successes were duly acknowledged:

> *Success of Garryowen Football Club in Munster Challenge Cup and Limerick Charity Cup.*
> *Success of relative in ploughing competition.*

Often, an 'in spite of' dimension made these achievements even more remarkable:

> *Employment obtained in spite of keen competition.*
> *Brother enabled to enter seminary in spite of many difficulties.*

The global scope of favours achieved added to our awe:

> *Safety of children on seashore (USA).*
> *Peace restored in home (Argentina).*
> *Marvellous escape of husband from death (China).*

When she had finished with the lists, mother conducted a spiritual educational quiz:

> Is it possible to hear Mass over the wireless?
> May a Catholic nurse send word to a non-Catholic minister that a non-Catholic patient, seriously ill, wishes to see him?
> How often should a Child of Mary who lives far away from any Centre be supposed to recite the Little Office of the Immaculate Conception?
> Is a dowry always necessary when a girl wishes to enter

a Religious Order?
Is company-keeping sinful?
In what part of the body does the soul exist?
What is the Church's attitude to mixed bathing?
If a sin were commmitted in a Church does this circumstance add to its guilt?
Do our dead friends know what is going on here on earth?
Is it right to subscribe to St Patrick's Guild?
Is it right to pray for a temporal favour such as, to win a share in the Sweepstakes?

I never heard a bad word pass my mother's lips but, being a devout follower of the Sacred Heart, in times of stress she'd often utter the pious ejaculations 'Sacred Heart of Jesus I place all my trust in you,' and 'Jesus, meek and humble of heart, make my heart like unto thine'. We always felt like little angels by bed time on Sunday night. On Monday we were as wild and bold as ever.

From 1957 to 1963, between the ages of six and eleven, I missed out on a lot of raza and queen cakes and spirituality, and did my time on Saturday and Sunday nights for my transgressions during the week. Publicly I took my punishments heroically and went off to bed as defiantly as any Spartan or defeated Jap. Privately, as I lay there all alone in the dark, I felt awfully sorry for myself, concluding that life was essentially unfair and that I had got a raw deal. My sins were sins of necessity: petty stealing of old scrap metal that was only rotting away — sure if the owners didn't want it 'twas a sin to leave it there and we in need of a few bob pocket money so badly; bullying — when it came to a choice between the polite pastimes of civilised children like going to the library and learning to play the piano or experimenting with my father's tools and messing about on the river or the railway line, which were out of bounds, I felt that the only way of ensuring that tell-tales didn't give the game away was by intimidation. Insubordination to parents and teachers was because I just could not keep my mouth shut when I knew they were wrong — like when my auntie Kitty, a chain-smoker, caught me smoking and I said that if it was bad for me 'twas much worse for her because she was old and smoked at least twenty fags a day. Or when my father told me to clean up after he had cut a load of firewood, I was annoyed, because he said I was too young to use the bow-saw and told him *he* had made the mess and could clean up himself.

I spent months rationalising and justifying my own position and eventually concluded that things would be much better if I were an only child like Beryl the Pearl or Oliver Twist. I'd be able to stuff myself with all the goodies in the house and wouldn't have to share them with anyone. All my relations would dote on me and give me money when my parents brought me round to show me off. I'd have a room full of toys at Christmas and at least six Easter eggs all to myself. My mother would be young and elegant and beautiful and would play bridge. My father, relaxing in his armchair by the fire, would browse through the latest travel magazine and suggest we go on a safari holiday next summer. And just when I was about to shoot a charging elephant, the rest trundled up the stairs and blew my sweet dreams away. Like the prince turned into a toad, I was back in 5, Rock Vale Terrace again, fighting to keep my own side of the bed.

I had to admit that the fantasy world was all right now and again but could become pretty boring. Here at home was reality, familiarity, security. Here you could take everything for granted. When my parents first saw this place 'twas miserable and grotty, but my father transformed it. All six of us children loved it and were blissfully unaware of our parents' mighty effort to maintain it as tenants, and eventually acquire it as a home of our own.

Where We Sported and Played

Rock Vale Terrace was a lane of six houses, up four steps off the main road. To the front and back were a door and window and behind was a tiny yard with an outdoor tap and toilet. Downstairs had a front room, a middle room and a kitchen. Upstairs was an attic with skylights back and front. The first time my mother saw the place she thought it was a dump, and she ran back to Shandon Street saying she'd never live there. But my father was young, idealistic, handy and determined to make it work. He set to and panelled the kitchen and hall walls to half-way with sheets of 8' x 4' plywood which I remember painted chocolate brown. The upper half to the ceiling was painted a matching cream. He sheeted all upstairs with ceiling board and divided it into two rooms. My mother was impressed with the transformation and agreed to try the place.

Every summer, while we were on holidays in Youghal, my father refurbished and redecorated, and the place improved in time. In 1956 he built a back-kitchen and a covered area across from the outdoor toilet where my mother did the washing. Often on a winter's morning he'd finish nightwork early, and our kitchen was the cosiest spot in all the world when we got up for school and he had the fire lighting and the porridge bubbling on the gas stove.

But I don't think my mother was ever really happy in Rock Vale. She always wanted a proper bathroom and a garden, and there were always problems with the roof. When repaired in one place it leaked somewhere else, and that went on for years. Despite my father's best efforts a total refurbishment was eventually needed. Mother decided to put her foot down and withhold the rent. Every Friday night father was shitless when the rent man came but mother was adamant. There'd be no more Mickey Mousing around with the job: she was leaving no workman up on that roof again to tinker around with bits of slate and cement; she wanted a proper job done or there'd be no rent, and that was that.

The rent man kept threatening but she remained undaunted, eventually dragging my father along to the landlord's solicitor to argue her case. When he said 'of course, Mr Delaney, you could make us an offer for the house,' my mother kicked my father under the table and said '£100'. They got it for £150. That was in 1969, and mother was very proud when she had the whole place refurbished with two lovely bedrooms upstairs and a proper bathroom downstairs. She got great satisfaction when everyone in the lane followed her example.

Occasionally the horror of her first sight of the place back in 1953 haunted her, and we nearly left once. After Anne was born in 1961 mother wasn't well and spent six weeks in hospital. My father was advised that a house near my grandmother's on the North side would help my mother recover and stay healthy, and we were allocated a new four-bedroomed house in Bantry Park Road by the Corporation. We were all packed and ready to go when Mother changed her mind out of consideration for my father, and the inconvenience it would cause him going to work at all times of the night during winter, and having to come down Fair Hill in all kinds of weather.

She was rewarded for her consideration, and there wasn't a bother on her until her mother died in 1986 and again the house began to haunt her. The sickness recurred a year later. When my father died suddenly in 1988 we were anxious that mother would leave and come to live near one of us. Now she felt it her duty to stay and that it wouldn't have been right to leave. But she couldn't stick it either. She only lasted a month. She never got that garden she longed for so much, but there are beautiful flowers growing on her grave in Kilcully.

2

PLAY

The Sacred Heart was called on to intervene often, for our playground, consisting of the quarry, the railway line, the Dublin Road and the Lee, was a mother's nightmare. Our house was four steps up a laneway, twenty yards from the main road. On a lovely June day in 1954, my sister Mai, then just one year old, was sitting strapped in her pram outside the house. As my mother came out the hall she saw pram and Mai and all career past the front door. The steps at the end of the lane saved her. The pram toppled over. There wasn't a bother on Mai, but we never found out what devil or demon released the brake.

Next to my mother's dread of the river was her fear of the railway, and Skinner had a lucky escape when he was fourteen months old. It was during the sugar beet season and he crept out onto the embankment to watch the gang of us as we waited excitedly with our big long sticks to knock stalks of beet out of the loaded wagons of the 'Youghal beet special'. Skinner became carried away by the spectacle and, unknown to us, crept out and along the track. He had gone too far by the time we noticed him and he sat back on his hunkers, waving his arms in the air with delight at the sound of the oncoming train. The driver braked, but it would take a quarter of a mile to stop a train-load of beet, and Skinner was under it, falling backwards just as it reached him. When the train finally ground to a halt we stood there frozen in horror, too shocked to cry. Then out crept Skinner from between the back wheels of the second last wagon and we raised our long sticks in the air with a spontaneous shout of relief and joy. We brought him home shoulder high as though we had just found Moses.

Where We Sported and Played

We were really convinced that it was the prompt action of his guardian angel, pushing him backwards just as the train met him, that saved Skinner. Reilly, our gang leader, was even more favoured with divine protection. Many a time we thought he was a goner but he always came through. On one occasion we built a club hut from waste galvanised sheeting and linoleum in the quarry, and Chief Reilly sent three of us braves to the high field to cut wooden poles to use as roof beams. We had been ordered to throw the poles spear-like to a designated spot in the quarry as we cut them. When I'd cut and stripped the fifth and final pole I gave it to Waddler, who was getting fed up of the hard work at this stage, and who consequently threw it somewhat carelessly in the general direction of the other poles. It ripped through the air towards Reilly's head 50 feet below while he, blissfully unaware, instructed some young aspirants in the ways of the brotherhood, as they sat around him on the grass. One of them was none too attentive and, when Reilly rose to give him a clatter, the pole embedded itself 6 inches deep dead centre in the patch where his arse had flattened the grass. It could have been his head.

That very same week he nearly met his Waterloo in the Lee. We were at the delicate stage in the exchange with the cook on a German cargo ship of a box of apples we had slogged in Montenotte for two packets of fags. There was general mistrust on both sides, the cook thinking we'd skidaddle with fags and apples, we thinking he'd tell us to feck off if we gave him the apples first. We eventually agreed to a simultaneous hand-over. Reilly, in his enthusiasm for the fags, overstretched himself, forgetting to calculate for the weight of the box of apples in his left hand, and down he went between ship and quay wall into 40 foot of water. Luckily for him 'twas full tide and almost level with the quayside. After a long five seconds he surfaced. Ricey grabbed him by the hair and, with one excited heave, landed him on *terra firma*. The German cook gave us a carton of Pall Mall, delighted to get rid of us quickly, and we could see him taking a huge slug from a brandy bottle as we made off down Water Street, listening to Reilly telling us how everything was green and how he could hear sweet music on his way to Davey Jones' Locker. But we knew he was only bulling

My cousin Sally had the greatest escape of all in the river. Against my mother's wishes Sally and her friend Dollie had gone for a spin in *The Lady Alice*, my father's 20 foot larch boat, at low tide. They became entangled in an old barge rope near the ferry slip, panicked and fell in. John Joe O'Malley was meant to be studying for exams in his room at home in Myrtle Hill overlooking the railway line and the river. Luckily for Sally he was more interested in observing the world go by outside than in his books. When he saw what was happening he cleared his garden wall, the railway line and the road in a flash and dragged Dollie out. As he did so he felt Sally at his feet and got her out too, just in time. Artificial respiration brought her around. We all gathered at the corner when the ambulance went down the road, as curious as any crowd at an accident when their own are not involved. When the shout came back that it was Sally who was in the river, women began to wring their hands, and shouts of 'Jesus, Mary and Joseph,' and 'O Mother of Divine God,' went up. Then we found out she was all right and things were back to normal in no time. My father recovered Sally's glasses at ebb tide next day and John Joe was a hero. All my Mother said by way of reprimand was 'you better get rid of that boat, Leo'. And he did. When he got another one five years later mother pretended not to know.

Our ingenuity in providing diversion for ourselves during the long school summer holidays bordered on the dangerous. Quite by accident we discovered that a tin bottle top placed on the railway line was flattened to the exact size and shape of a penny. We decided to go into big time racketeering. American style penny bubble-gum machines were all the rage. There were three on the Lower Road and two at St Luke's Cross on the way to school. We decided to use our friends from St Luke's as decoys, and gave them a bag of our specially minted coins telling them that St Luke's was their turf and they were entitled to clean the joint out. They fell for it. We milked the three on the Lower Road dry and, when a parental enquiry got under way, protested our innocence and blamed the St Luke's crowd. If there were tell-tale signs with bubble-gum stuck to bedclothes afterwards mothers weren't informing on their own children, and balls of the stuff were used as currency to trade for comics, catapults and birds' eggs for weeks afterwards.

Sometimes, under outside influence, we overstepped the mark. Rusty, recently come from England, had just been initiated into the gang when he intimated to Reilly that he had a novel scheme for acquiring free sweets. An impromptu council was held and Rusty explained his plan. Roycrofts had two separate entrances to the hardware and grocery stores, with the latter containing a vast range of irresistible goodies, from penny sweets like Peggy's legs, gob stoppers and black jacks to shilling bars of Cadbury's chocolate, boxes of Black Magic and Toblerones, all displayed enticingly in impregnable glass cases on top of huge solid mahogany counters. Rusty, with his English-trained eye, had noticed that the glass cases were not an integral part of the counter and could be eased ever so gently forward, thus enabling someone on someone else's back to have access to the box of Toblerones on the bottom shelf.

'A piece of cake,' he said.

'No way,' I immediately protested, 'no way! That's real stealing, not like taking scrap metal or a few apples from a tree with loads. No way! That's real stealing.'

Waddler said he was opting out too, 'because a box of

Toblerones would last a whole year in a shop, and if it's gone in a week someone is bound to find out and then we're all up shit creek.'

No good. The majority applied the whip and that was that. On Monday and Tuesday we cased the joint and, on Wednesday, two of us went into the hardware to buy the cheapest effective item we could think of as a decoy — a Brillo scour pad, located on one of the higher shelves, and thus requiring a ladder and the secondment of the assistant from the grocery. With split-second timing the other two went in the other door. One went piggy-back. The glass case was eased out, Toblerones taken and glass case eased back in twenty seconds. They were almost back in the quarry before we had paid for the Brillo pad.

We divided the bars between us. I didn't enjoy them. I had never eaten Toblerone before and it is an acquired taste. I thought the specky white things were bits of mould and that 'twas the lousiest chocolate I ever tasted. Every bite was a bite of guilt. I'm sure the others felt the same but they wouldn't give me the soot of it, and they munched away to the end like the old eejit of a philosopher in Greece who drank the poison as though it were a nice cool drink on a hot summer's day. When I came home to tea I felt really guilty and knew I had to make some effort at restitution. So I gave my mother the Brillo pad, saying I found it on the road. She was delighted, said it was very thoughtful of me, and gave me a penny. O my sick soul! The web of sin was closing in around me and for the first time in my life I eagerly waited for Saturday to come in order to go to confession. 'Twas the longest few days I ever put down. One bite of Toblerone now and all the guilt comes back.

Some of our other summer holiday activities were also in dubious taste. Frog races in the quarry pond in July were great *craic* but had to be indulged in discreetly because of the cruelty of the game. Catching frogs was no bother. They could be found in their hundreds in the moss and the wet grass under the cliff face. Making them race in straight lines was a different matter. They went all over the place, so jumping races were out. But frogs are good swimmers and after we had doctored them they could only swim in straight lines. Each of us got a lolly stick and numbered it, mine was always five. Up the frog's arse and out it's mouth and it certainly wasn't going to jump. But it improved his breast stroke, making him spread even wider, and that in a straight line too. When the race was over it was over. No frog could be retained. There was no such thing as a champion, which made it kind of unique. The stick was removed and off they jumped, apparently no more frightened than they always looked.

One day I caught a beauty. A big lump of a bull-frog with a speckled rough back like a crocodile. He looked ferocious altogether with the stick up through him, rearing to go like a witch on a broomstick. The race itself was a non-event. The others were no match for him. Understandably, I was reluctant to part with him and placed him under a jam jar, stick and all, while I went to discuss the matter with Reilly, who was already busy in the miniature jungle looking for an ape of a frog the likes of mine. 'A rule is a rule, and that's that,' was all he said. If the frog was under another jar things might have been different, but the sooner my fella was released, the sooner Reilly knew he had a chance of recapturing him himself. I went back to the jar reluctantly and gawked in stupefaction. The jar was in smithereens, the brute gone. This guy was some frog! He had rocked the jar till it toppled and broke against a stone and, stick or no stick up his arse, he had skidaddled.

Consternation and panic broke out among the gang. This fella would blow our cover if found by someone else. 'You'd better find him or we're all knackered,' says Reilly, and we formed a posse and moved methodically in a line through the grass towards the cliff. Too late. From the little plateau above us where all the women gathered to recite the Rosary as a protection against polio, the prayerful murmur was shattered by, 'O Jesus Mary and Joseph!' as the brute, twice as horrific with stick intact, perched on Mrs Gogan's leg. We were caught redhanded. Our mothers were so shocked by our cruelty that all they could say by way of reprimand was, 'How could ye do such a thing like that to one of God's creatures?' and, after a short pause, continued with the Rosary. That was in 1957, and by the time I made my First Communion a year later, I knew that such mutilation was sinful.

We didn't feel the same about crabs. They didn't look half as sad or as human as frogs. In fact they looked more like mechanical machines than creatures. We fished them out with bits of cheese attached to safety pins at the ferry slip, and reckoned that any creature that was so greedy as to keep a hold of the cheese till it got caught did not deserve sympathy. We put numbers on their backs with nails dipped in red lead and lined them up at the side of the Dublin Road. 'Twas more an obstacle course than a race track — the one that made it first to the other side without being crushed was deemed the winner. If more than one survived we went into limitation stakes and, in true gladiatorial spirit, they were sent to and fro until only one survived. The numbers were absolutely necessary because crabs never walk in a straight line and the fella who started in the left lane, if he survived the traffic, could end up going scew-ways in a circle around the cat's eyes in the middle of the road. The winner was given a big lump of cheese and returned to a hole in the slob. If a champion was ever fished out again he was never raced. He had survived and beaten fate, on luck not on merit. We would have been denying good luck if we made him run the gauntlet again.

Progress destroyed this game for, as traffic volumes increased, the level of enjoyment and carnage became unacceptable. There were very few winners and a lot of frustrated trainers. Three days in succession we raced them, and not one survived: the first day a bus and a lorry obliterated the lot on the first leg; the second day two survivors contesting the second leg bit the dust under a Corporation steam-roller. On the third day Waddler's boy nearly made it. 'Twas between himself and Reilly's. A Ford Chevrolet taxi blew Reilly's boy away, but Waddler's survived a hectic and stormy crossing, and was only 4 feet from the kerb when a CIE delivery horse kicked the shite out of him. Waddler freaked and threw a stone at the horse. The horse bolted and kicked the door of a new Ford Anglia. The driver made a mad dash after us and slipped on a squashed crab. We made a bolt for it up the quarry. When the commotion died down crab-racing was banned by parental order. We weren't too disappointed. It had run it's course and time had caught up with it.

Chocolate crumb was a seasonal delicacy of ours during the summer months. Big rocks of raw chocolate were made in Cadbury's factory in Rathmore, Co. Kerry, and brought by rail to Cork for shipment to England and refinement into the shop product which we didn't think nearly as nice. If you hung around the quayside long enough a docker might take pity on you and throw you a lump or two, and if you were lucky he might ask you to go to the shop for five Woodbines and he'd give you a handful in return. I detested playing the *béal bocht*, getting scraps out of sympathy, and decided to organise a hobble. While the dockers, crane men and CIE men took their lunch on the quay wall we sneaked up the other side of the wagons to the one farthest away, broke the seal on the big iron bolt, turned the heavy handle a full 180 degrees, slid the bolt, opened the door, slit the bottom bag, and out poured the lovely lumps of chocolate, like the gold in *The Count of Monte Cristo*. Then we made a mad run for it to the main road and back to the quarry to stuff ourselves. Later that afternoon we realised that, in our excitement, we had forgotten to close the wagon door to cover our tracks, and had blown our chances of repeating the operation.

No matter what we tried afterwards it didn't work, because one of the CIE gangers who had it in for us always ate his lunch by the railway wall, in full view of the road and the siding of the wagons. We couldn't get the better of him though we tried all sorts of manoeuvres: sneaking from sleeper to sleeper between the tracks, underneath the wagons was no good. The wagons were too high and there wasn't enough cover. Coming up the river in a punt in against the quay wall didn't work either. He caught us as we made the mad dash across the fifteen feet of open ground between the quay wall and the wagons. He really had us pinned down, and he knew it. It was really beginning to bug me. I was determined not to let him best me, and stayed awake half the night trying to devise a plan to beat him. No good. Things went from bad to worse and I was getting into trouble at school as well. The teacher knew I was miles away and he'd often pounce on me with a question out of the blue. Sometimes I'd take a chance and bluff my way out of it, but I really blew it one day when he asked who read the Proclamation outside the GPO in 1916 and I replied, 'Hitler'. That earned me eight slogs. I was about to concede that the ganger had me beaten. I decided to give myself until Saturday to come up with something spectacular, but by Monday I would definitely be turning over a new leaf, chocolate crumb or no chocolate crumb.

We went to see *The Great Train Robbery* in the Pavilion on Saturday. Half-way through I got excited and shouted, 'ha, ha, me boyo, I have ye now!' and an usher shone her torch menacingly in our direction. At least I knew how Einstein must have felt when he discovered $E=MC^2$ and I told the lads my plan on the way home. I slept like a log that night and at Mass next morning asked for St Anthony's help — not to get the chocolate crumb, that wouldn't have been right and he'd have shot me down anyway, but for

35

fair play and a bit of a break in my personal confrontation with the CIE Goliath. The gang were on red alert awaiting the next train-load of chocolate crumb, and when it arrived I gave the orders.

Waddler and Murphy made the usual approach up the quay towards the siding from the east side. Ricey and myself continued up the road intending to double back near St Patrick's church and make our way along the quay from the west a little later. When Waddler and Murphy got within 100 yards of the wagons they pretended to hide and sneak along the wall. Your man spotted them, as expected, and began to roar and shout to frighten them off. They were under orders to hold tight, lie low for a minute or two and continue their approach. Your man fell for it and now he stood up shaking his fist at them. They held tight for another while, advanced again to within fifty yards of him, just outside firing range. Now he got really mad and started to throw rocks at them. Still they manoeuvred closer and closer to the last wagon on the east side. Finally he lost his cool altogether and left his post, throwing rocks after them all the way down the quay. When he stopped, they stopped and began to sneak back like brazen cats who couldn't resist the temptation. Bit by bit he was lured all the way around the corner at Water Street and out of sight.

Meanwhile, we made our approach from the west, and the hobble itself was a piece of cake. It was all over in a minute and a half and we made our retreat back towards St Patrick's again with a shopping bag full of chocolate crumb. Full or not it didn't matter. We had won and there was your man half-way down the Lower Road, like a madman throwing rocks at schoolboys. He finally realised that there was something amiss and ran back to find his worst fears confirmed. I deliberately left the wagon doors open so that he would realise that he'd been had the minute he came around the corner, and the picture of dismay on his face was sweeter than any chocolate crumb.

Where We Sported and Played

Our journey to the quarry was like Caesar's triumphant return from Gaul. The bag was admired in awe and wonder as though it contained Hannibal's head. We were heroes who, against all the odds, brought home the spoils. I benignly threw handfuls of chocolate crumb here and there and all the children scampered after them. By this time the following had thronged to a procession that couldn't be dispersed discreetly without drawing the attention of my mother. 'So that's where my shopping bag went to,' says she, looking inside and seeing the stolen treasure. She dumped it all out on the ground, threw lumps of it in the air shouting, 'all a ba', and dragged me off by the scruff of the neck saying, 'That's that. When you go back to school next week there'll be no more doing as you please. No more being a big shot with the lads or getting everything you put your eye on. I'll put a stop to your gallop yet, me boy.' That was the final indignity: to have felt like Caesar one minute and Job the next.

Reilly's greatest claim to fame was that he was cox of the boat club's *Eileen a Leanna*, and he attempted to bring his position of authority on the river to the road. His box-car was always a foot longer than everyone else's. His brother worked in the dockyard so his front axle was always properly suspended and his bearings well oiled. As a matter of course he held the land speed record for formula one box-cars on Lyon's Lane. If anyone tried to challenge him he was full of subtle diversions to impress and divert the mob: sticking lolly sticks in the wheels to simulate motorised sound or ingratiating himself with the youngsters by getting them to hold on to his shoulders and scooter along for the first few yards of a ride. He arrived one day all full of himself, like a returned Yank, with the seat of a Morris Minor bolted to the frame, and he perched there like the bishop on Confirmation day. He was up to his 'Alexander the Great' stuff again. If 'twas cowboys and

Indians Reilly was always the sheriff; if 'twas boats he was the captain; if 'twas hurling he was Christy Ring. And here he was now, Sterling Moss, expecting us to be the pit mechanics at his every beck and call. I'd had enough. 'Feck this for a lark,' says I. 'What about size, shape and rules of construction and design?'

'This is a new game,' says he, 'we're all going for sumped up models from now on.'

'Right,' says I, and off I went in a huff.

I waited for Waddler and Murphy at the corner of our lane and told them that they were my pit team, that the Fisheries' Grand Prix was on. I needed them both more than they knew: Murphy had an old Pedigree pram discarded in the yard, and Waddler had got a new bathroom and wouldn't have any more use for the 6 foot zinc bath in the back. Early on Saturday morning both pram and bath were moved to the quarry. By the time Mrs Murphy came to claim her bath back it was too late. Four 4-inch nails fastened it to a 6' x 6" x 1" tongued and grooved sheet which formed the chassis of our new machine, and Waddler's pram could never be put together again after a cold chisel and hammer had separated the axles from the body. One of the three galvanised rubbish bins outside Casey's shop was procured and split in two to form the bonnet. We painted her bottle-green that evening and streaked the name *Green Lightning* in bold red lead across the bonnet.

I decided that O'Mahony's Avenue, a steep incline linking the Lower Road with the top of Summerhill, was the ideal spot for a test drive. The ridged surface, originally designed to facilitate horse-drawn traffic in frosty weather, would be an ideal test of the stability of the frame and the capability of the rubber-spoked wheels. I had schooled Murphy and Waddler in the act of ballast. They piled in the back and I took the steering rope. But my elementary physics were not enough and O'Mahony's

Where We Sported and Played

Avenue proved an unfortunate choice. We made a most graceful start. The ridged concrete surface and the weight of the two on the back axle kept her slow. But the gathering momentum proved too much for my young brother John who, in panic, let go the stay rope. The vibrations from the ridges increased and, like a rodeo cowboy, I hung on to the ineffective steering. The strain proved too much for the 4 inch nails. The steering rope broke. The bath ground to a halt on its side with us still inside, and the chassis flew off in a tangent and somersaulted into a horse trough. Murphy lost the sole of his shoe and Waddler was holding his thigh to convince himself it was still there. The only tentative link the chassis still had with the body was the tangled ball of wool attached to one of its protruding 4 inch nails, and the top half of my school jumper.

Reilly laughed in derision. But we still had five days and I'd put the smile on the other side of his face yet. It was back to the drawing-board. We made considerable modifications. The 1 inch square cross-piece to which the front axle was attached we replaced with an ash shovel handle, and liberally greased the suspending bolt, giving something of the effect of power steering. We added two other handles to the main frame of the chassis for balance, doubled its strength by adding another tongued and grooved sheet and bolted down the bath. This time 'twas all or nothing. We were going down with her if we had to.

The august surrounds of Trafalgar Hill in Lower Montenotte was our Monte Carlo for Saturday's Grand Prix. If our name for the course 'The Blood Track', was somewhat out of keeping with its ambiance, it was singularly apt to describe the treacherously smooth tarmacadam and hairpin bends that led off the main Dublin Road at Tivoli, to the *hoi poloi* residential area that ran up from the hill-top to the junction of the main road.

Green Lightning looked immaculate in all her reinforcement and the rest didn't look too bad either. An array of exotically-christened machines barricaded the hill: Blakes from Beale's Hill had the *Brown Bomber;* Mahers from the Square had *Ragusa;* Beausangs from Castle View had *U-Tant;* Joyces from Fish Lane, *Santa Maria de la Rosa* and Clarkes from MacCurtain Street, *The Foggy Dew.* But Reilly's dream machine was the only one I really wanted to beat. He had cheated again. His *Sputnik* had been built by his brothers. It was painted a dazzlingly daring red and had pumped up CIE baggage-truck wheels emblazoned with flashy spike chrome accessories. This was only a two-man race.

After all the preparation and display the race itself was a bit of a let-down. The start was by gentleman's agreement but Reilly did the dirty on me on the grid. He had seen the film *Ben Hur* and horsed himself into poll position by using some of the also-rans as spoilers to hem me in. I copped on straight away and instructed Waddler to use my hurley to fend off the *Brown Bomber* and *Ragusa* before the first hairpin. On the next straight we built up steam and, when the *Santa Maria de la Rosa* came across our bows, we met her broadside and blew her into a drain. Around the next hairpin and there in front of us was *The Foggy Dew.* I threw my jumper at the driver and they enveloped a telegraph pole. One bend, one straight and Reilly's *Sputnik* to go.

Waddler used the hurley to give us extra propulsion and we were on Reilly's tail coming out of the bend. Neck and neck in the straight now. *Sputnik* blew a tyre on a grating and went into a wobble. His chrome spikes entangled in our back wheel and neither of us reached the finish line. They careered off to the left and scythed through the daffodils, frightening a red setter so badly that he was never any good as a gun dog again. We lost our right front wheel and skidded along the footpath off the main road, finally coming to a halt against the front door of a brand new maroon-coloured Ford Cortina, which the owner was proudly showing off to his neighbours. He was so horrified that he almost cried. We were so relieved to be alive that we burst out laughing.

The lads took it for granted that Reilly had a natural right to be gang leader. I was beginning to get a bit pissed off by this presumption, and beginning to lose faith in some of his more corny schemes like his efforts to get us free from school after lunch by putting blotting paper in our shoes to make us faint, or holding our boots under drain pipes to convince our mothers that it was too wet to send us back. 'Twas all too cumbersome, uncomfortable and dramatic for my liking. 'Twould have been easier just to go on the lang. Reilly's judgment was suspect too, and he hadn't a clue how to pick a team. When he was captain, 'Above the Bridge' beat us on three successive occasions. As well as that I was getting rightly fed up of always being a horse whenever we played cowboys and Indians.

One day when I dared to question the route by which he led us to school and insisted that there was another at least as short, he had me punished in the quarry. Ricey and Murphy held me while he put a lighted paper under my chin. I never flinched or cried or kicked. Ricey and Murphy admitted afterwards, without exactly putting it in these terms, that they felt like the Centurion at the Crucifixion and that truly I was a brave man. Had Reilly known his Machiavelli he would have realised that the only way to subdue an insubordinate is to exterminate him and, now that the lads perceived me as an alternative leader, his end came more quickly than he expected.

On Saturdays during autumn we went on expeditions to Woodhill House, familiarly known as 'The Haunted'. Though a mere half-mile from the Lower Road, the august surrounds of the once glorious estate were to us another country, and although now considerably overgrown, the grounds still retained some vestiges of their former glory, with their magnificent walks bordered by red and mauve rhododendron, laurel and yew running all the length of the red brick boundary wall. The splendid white rose tree, that bloomed before other rose trees even showed buds and remained in bloom right into the following winter, still stands on the lower walk. The big knotted eating chestnut tree remains as well, as does a huge 120 foot high pine, which we believed was the tallest tree in Ireland.

The house itself belonged to the Quaker, Cooper Penrose (after whom Penrose Quay is named), who was High Sheriff of Cork two hundred years ago. In our time only the skeleton of the once beautiful mansion remained, with its elegant terrazzo floor and bits of marble staircase as reminders of its former glory. The whole place was awesome and fascinating, and we bathed in the lingering atmosphere of its grandeur. It came as no surprise to me to read the following description in later years:

The Woodhill grounds were spacious and splendid. The beautifully kept lawns were surrounded by trees, and sculptures were dispersed throughout. The 'Philosopher's Walk', which was bounded by a wall of red brick, was adorned with domes containing antique bronze busts. This walk ran from just inside the main entrance gate on what later became Lover's Walk to where the Penrose property met Belleview, the property of the Nicholsons.

Cooper Penrose had a passionate love of art, and he possessed such numerous pictures accommodated in a specially-built wing of his home, that Woodhill became known as 'The Irish Vatican'.

The windows of this art gallery were made of pure Venetian stained glass. It is said that the special wing was intended for a consignment of sculpture from Italy but the ship bearing it sank, and so the extension be-

*came a picture gallery. On the extensive grounds
sloping down to the shore and the narrow roadway at
Tivoli stood many statues, bronze and marble, which
Cooper Penrose brought back from his European
tours....*

*The interior of Woodhill was a place of splendour.
The staircase was of elaborate, intricately designed
wrought iron, with marble steps and richly carpeted,
being wide enough for a 'carriage and pair' to mount.
The fireplaces had leaden surrounds and bronze
ornamentations. Magnificent cut-glass chandeliers
hung from the ceilings of Italian architecture in
ballroom and drawing-rooms.* (Catherine M. Herbert,
Evening Echo, 7 August, 1974.)

All we knew of the history of the place was that Sarah
Curran stayed here. We firmly believed that 'bould'
Robert Emmet used to make his way here secretly to meet
her and barely escaped from the Redcoats once or twice,
and that only by swimming the Lee all the way down to
Blackrock — and that after Emmet's execution in 1803 poor
Sarah pined away and died. 'Twas she now, wandering
around the place dressed all in white, like a lost soul, continually weeping for her dead lover, who gave the awful
eerie feeling to the place. So we knew the place as 'The
Haunted', not Woodhill, House.

Some of that was true of course: Sarah did stay here,
but only after Emmet's execution in 1803, and here she met a
British officer, Captain Robert Henry Sturgeon, whom she
married in Glanmire Church on 24 November 1805. And
Emmet, though a patriot, was no athlete, and it is extremely unlikely that a puny *padhsán* like him could have
swum the Lee.

Historic fact may shatter the heroic romantic myth,
but there was no denying the spookiness of the place. There
is an explanation for this too. Just inside the railway wall

on the Tivoli side of Woodhill is a funny-looking tower about 16 feet high. Reliable sources claim that beneath this secluded miniature tower is a hollow, deep enough for a leaden casket to be inserted in a perpendicular position. Cooper Penrose died in 1815 at the age of seventy-six and exhaustive research has failed to establish where he was buried. My father was convinced, and he had it on good authority from older residents, that Cooper Penrose was buried in the tower and, as evidence, used to quote an alleged statement of his 'as long as a Penrose stands at Woodhill nobody will build on the right of way'.

By an order dated 18 May 1989 Cork Corporation granted permission for the demolition of the remains of the Penrose mansion and the construction of a luxury dwelling on the original site. The schedule contains the following conditions:

> *Prior to the demolition of any part of the existing structure, a fully detailed photographic and drawing survey and record, in accordance with the requirements of and to the satisfaction of the Planning Authority, and the Irish Architectural Archive, shall be made of the structure and copies of such survey and record shall be made available to the Planning Authority and also to the Irish Architectural Archive. A landscaping schedule for the site which makes provision for (a) the retention of existing trees on site to the maximum extent; (b) new tree planting to be carried out in the first planting season after occupancy of the dwelling shall be submitted to and agreed with the Planning Authority prior to the commencement of development.*

That's grand but did anybody tell the new owner anything about the tower or Cooper Penrose's alleged statement?

Before the game of cowboys and Indians on Saturday it was generally agreed that we needed a new arms supply.

Where We Sported and Played

Our ash bows had dried out and no longer had sufficient spring, while what was left of our sleek hazel arrows had become too brittle. The grounds of Myrtle Hill house would afford us a ready supply and, like the committed braves we were, we headed off down along the railway line. The house adjacent had been recently purchased by the county librarian who was attending to his overgrown garden, and he looked on us benignly as he thought we were headed for the wastelands of 'The Haunted' and 'The Scheme'. Our enthusiastic and ecstatic shouts of 'here's a beauty', 'give us a hand with this whopper here', 'don't be sticking them arrows in me eye, ye gowl, ye', drew the attention of the newly-arrived librarian, who was horrified and enraged by our barbarity and vandalism. As he approached, Reilly sounded the retreat. They all scattered. I didn't. This was our turf and no newly-arrived settler was going to deprive us of our inheritance.

'What do you mean by cutting those young saplings?'

'The sticks, is it?'

'Why are you breaking all those young ash and hazel rods?'

'To make bows and arrows.'

'And who gave you permission to come in here?'

'Mind your own business and I'll mind mine.'

'Do you think you have the right to go around destroying nature at will?'

'No but ...'

'This is uncivilised conduct.'

'But we always ...'

'No more buts and have some regard and appreciation for the beauty of nature that surrounds you.'

'I suppose ...'

'Now clear off out of here before you do any more damage and I have to call the guards.'

Though I was chastened by this lecture when I rejoined the gang I could see the general admiration for the fact

45

that I had stood my ground, and although Reilly was automatically elected sheriff for the afternoon game, he knew that I was ready to challenge.

We were on opposite sides for the game. He was with the garrison defending the house, I with the force attacking from the cover of the wood. We all started in the clearing with seven a side and made for our positions, counting out loud '5, 10, 15, 20 ... 100', and the game was on. They had taken up firing positions in the first and second storey windows to the front and sides and had us pinned down in the trees. Waddler and Murphy played the hero and ploughed through the high grass to the front. They hadn't a chance, and weren't gone five yards when Ricey blew them indisputably away. Another of our braves was shot out of a tree when a startled pigeon gave his position away. Stalemate for about a minute, and then Ricey, thinking we were all in the long grass, left his front window and came at us to finish it off quickly. He came further and further before realising we weren't there. Then he panicked and tried to run back to his window. Bully got him in the back but in his excitement exposed himself to their left window and he came a cropper as well.

Only Rusty and myself were left and they didn't know where we were. We withdrew further back and encircled wide to get at them from behind. I made it to the back of the house easily enough but Rusty was spotted near the stables and Reilly picked him off. 'Twas four to one now and I felt really heroic. I crouched behind the back wall and could see them gesticulating to each other, from which I concluded that they thought I was accompanying Rusty, and Reilly was pompously insisting 'he's mine'. I leapt over the wall, through a basement window, up the stairs to the first landing and shot three of them in the back as they covered the front. As I came through the window one of Reilly's dead buddies beckoned to him and, as I reached the top of the stairs, he shouted 'bang, bang, you're dead, forty bullets in your head', but he was miles too late and no way could he have shot me then from his vantage point in the stables. I disputed the call and he came down in a fury. The game was truly over now.

Those who had been shot dead for a while had been bored stiff but were now quickened to life with renewed interest in the the real fight. Reilly swung me around by the shoulder and I slipped on the mossy floor. 'Now,' he says, 'when I say you're dead, you're dead'.

I got up, pushed him and replied, 'Watch it. Who do you think you are, anyhow?'

'So ye want a fight, do ye?' says he, poking a straight left into my face and splitting my lip.

The gang formed a ring around us and there, in what had been the magnificent ballroom of Woodhill House, we set to. We boxed around, sizing each other up at a distance at first. My straight left drew blood from his nose. A clash of heads and my left eye puffed up. We punched and pushed and groaned trading blow for blow. Advantage swayed as we each gave way occasionally. Then we tired and began to grunt and pant. When I slipped he pounced in close, stood over me and hit me before I could get up. I bucked and in a wild fury threw a haymaker of a right, catching him on the chin and driving him back. He was out on his feet and I kept pumping straight lefts into his face. He peddled backwards but they pulled me off just before he toppled through an open window. 'Twas all over on a TKO.

It must have been the strangest post-fight atmosphere ever. Everyone was stunned as the enormity of what had happened sank in. The ancient régime had been overthrown. We lit a fire in the basement and sat around just staring into it. No one told ghost stories or suggested any games, as we used to do on other occasions. I had an awful *tocht* on me and was close to tears. I knew that privately now they all held me in great esteem. I was terribly mixed up and, in some sad way, realised that Reilly was only human too and that another myth of invincibility had been shattered. We were despondent going home, not bothering to bring our bows and arrows with us. Some of the lads talked about joining a swimming club up town. 'Twas the end of an era and Monday would see a new régime.

Even the river wasn't going Reilly's way any longer. The regatta was dying, and he was getting too big to be cox anyway. When Dean Sexton's boxing club was founded in 1959 it was to be his last hurrah. For a week before opening night we spoke about nothing else. Floyd Patterson had just regained the world heavyweight title and old copies of *Ring Magazine* stolen from barbers' shops were compulsory reading at every corner of the Lower Road. We were all heroes of the next rags to riches story, all rearing to go. Experts in the rough and tumble of the street fight, all we wanted was to be allowed up and at 'em and beat our way to fame.

Like a herd of buffalo on the rampage, all bravado, we crowded into the boat club, now a make-shift gym, at 7.30 on Monday evening. We were immediately taken aback by the strict regimentals. First we were screened, asked if we had our parents' permission, checked out medically, weighed, and sent to stand in a row at the top of the hall where the trainer would talk to us. 'Twas the old story of life versus art. He told us to stop dreaming and get the lead out, that if any of us were there for the *craic* we could forget it, that none of us was going to win a Munster title in a few weeks, that we'd get nowhere without training and discipline. Then he outlined the programme for Mondays, Wednesdays and Fridays: 7 rounds of skipping, 2 rounds of shadow boxing, 2 rounds of ground work and 3 rounds of sparring. If we were really serious about going places we should go to bed early, get up early, eat plenty of fresh vegetables and give up the fags.

All of that took the wind out of our sails and I couldn't help thinking that I'd have more *craic* as a novice in the

Christian Brothers. A box of assorted gloves, discarded by the army, was then produced and we were paired off and shown how to shape up to each other. Reilly, as usual, was cock of the walk and he strutted around tapping his gloves together and making little shadow shimmies and twirls, as though he had been doing this all his life. Then they all began to ape him and things got out of hand, with fellas throwing all kinds of unorthodox punches from every conceivable angle in a totally uncoordinated way. We were called to order, told how to stand sideways, feet apart for balance, to keep chin and right elbow tucked in for protection, to lead with the left and side-step out of trouble. We weren't nearly as active then and just stood there like seized-up machines stuck to the ground. 'Now that shook ye,' said the trainer, 'get it into yer heads that ye have a long way to go before any of ye win anything. That's enough for tonight. Wednesday 7.30.' There were forty-two of us the first night. Only eighteen came back.

On Sunday 6 March 1964 I won the Munster Juvenile Schoolboy Championship at 6 stone, and was due to fight for the national title in Dublin during Easter week. The finals clashed with the Corporation Scholarship examinations for which my father and mother thought I was a dead cert. I knew that I had only the remotest chance of winning a scholarship and played this one so cutely that it was on my conscience for a long time afterwards. I insisted at home that I wanted to do the scholarship examination, but hinted that the thought of having been deprived of an opportunity to represent my club, city and province in the National Stadium would play on my mind so much that I would be unable to concentrate on the exam, and would thus miss out on both. My parents consulted with my teacher and reluctantly consented to allow me go to Dublin.

We left Cork at 7.00am on a crisp bright April morning in order to be in the Stadium before 12.00 noon for weigh-in. We boxers had fasted since the night before in order to hold

to our respective weights and were physically and emot-
ionally drained by all the preliminaries. It wasn't at all
like the hype, the hero worship and the glory we had seen
on the big screen. Hassled officials of the IABA growled at
club secretaries about incorrectly-filled entry forms. Trainers haggled about the uneven floor under the scales. In one
corner two boxers were skipping, sweating profusely in an
effort to shed an extra pound or two. The building itself
was dismal and cold, and we were weak with hunger by
the time we got out of the place at 1.45pm.

Then they took us to the Castle Hotel for the finest
meal I ever had in my life. I have never been back since but
have often passed that building and have done so with
reverence and affection, for no hotel meal I've ever had
anywhere since has ever surpassed it. After the cold
concrete and steel of the Stadium I really appreciated the
warmth and welcome of the red carpet, the solid silver
cutlery and starched linen table cloth.

We had chicken soup to start with in big white china
plates with a gold rim. I can still taste the delicious thick,
clear broth with real lumps of chicken, chopped carrot and
peas. Roast beef was the main course: thick tender slices in
tangy brown gravy, with more fresh peas and crunchy
carrots and rakes and rakes of delicious big chips. We
finished off with fresh fruit salad. The pep was back in us
and we were all fighting fit again.

Afterwards we retired to our digs to relax and lie down
and allow all this luxurious food convert itself to energy.
We rose at six, picked up our gear and headed for the
Stadium. I was paired against the Connaught champion in
the semi-final, an awkward flat-footed, hard-hitting
individual from Loughrea. But he had no savvy. I kept him
at long range during the first round, picking him off with
straight lefts and right crosses. He became frustrated in
the second round and made a few mad lunges at me. I side-
stepped the first two but stood my ground on the third and

caught him smack on the cheek with a right cross, followed by a left hook on his way down, and that was him on his way back to Loughrea.

It wasn't as easy the next night in the final against the Leinster champion who had won the title the previous year. I decided to give it a lash from the start. For all his experience I had him in trouble in the first round and 'twas half-way through the second before he adjusted his style to cope with the onslaught. He began to out-fox and out-box me then and got on top slowly. But I still came at him in the third and final round with all guns blazing and my hands going like two well-oiled pistons. His ring craft won it for him on a majority decision. I lost but felt great, knowing I could mix it with the best of them. That was a lesson as good as any scholarship to carry to secondary school with me.

SCHOOL

Come September parents were relieved that we were back at school and someone else's responsibility for part of the day. Psyching up began a week in advance: 'you're going to be a big boy now'; 'the teacher will be delighted with ye and she'll tell ye lovely stories'; 'and what will I do at all without a great little boy like you around the place?' All this 'Wee Hughie' crap was meant to fool me into wanting to go, but it didn't. I knew that my mother was relieved to have another demon off her hands and, instead of fearing for me in the tough world outside, she really hoped that the experience would tame me. I was as reluctant as any young fledgling to fly the nest and, when the *plámás* had no effect on me, was told to 'shut up out a dat or I'll give ye a clip around the ear a ye'. The fact of the matter was that I was scared out of my shite at the prospect and felt that the young Alexander the Great or Marco Polo would have baulked at the epic journey we had to undergo from the Fisheries to Ballyhooley Road.

We started at the Oriental bar, proceeded quickly through the hostile territory above the Railway Bridge, then the steep incline of Grattan's Hill and O'Mahony's Avenue, past the sinister Protestant national school and the splendid edifice of St Luke's Church of Ireland. An army officer stood there and waved to the Protestant children as they entered. On my first day I thought he had been placed there to protect them from us who, in the spirit of the Crusades, might have been inspired to attack them. In time I realised that he was just a Protestant Irish army officer who brought his children to school every morning. Next was the busy crossroads of: Montenotte, Wellington Road,

Where We Sported and Played

Ballyhooley Road and Gardiners Hill. Here was a veritable bazaar with an ornate stone horse trough and a little building that looked like a cross between a sentry box and a pagoda, which now serves as a sort of sophisticated newspaper stall in the middle of the road. On one side was a branch of Cudmore's fruit and sweet shops with an elegant window display of exotica such as pineapples and dates, which we only ever saw in films — and in black and white at that. Hennessy's wines and spirits and tea merchants was on the other side with its beautifully ornate varnished façade and polished samovar in the window. The strange, pleasant aroma of snuff and tobacco that wafted on the crisp autumnal air on that first morning in September 1956 has never gone stale. A veritable school of life to inform our eyes, ears and noses ringed the crossroads: a shoemaker, a confectioner, a pub, a bookie, a chemist and a post office. A hedge school was all that was needed to analyse the sensory experience. Socrates and Plato would have thrived on such an academy and you could stuff your formal schooling. School was nothing but a museum compared to this.

On my first day I was put sitting next to a fella named Dan from the Barracks. He wore black boots and had a right old-fashioned country look about him. There wasn't a bother on me, but this poor devil was completely flabbergasted by the whole scene. *Goldilocks and the Three Bears* proved too much for him. When the teacher growled '"Who has been eating my porridge?" said the baby bear,' poor little Dan became hysterical and his big sister in first class had to be sent for. She calmed him down and he explained that he was afraid the bears would get him because his mother, sister and himself had eaten their three bowls of porridge that morning. He was grand then for a while but threw another tantrum when he heard *Red Riding Hood*. He was convinced the big bad wolf would get his sister and himself going through the Glen on the way home, and so she had to take the long way around.

Where We Sported and Played

Our teacher, Miss Byrne, kept discipline. When she said *tá* we all had to say *tá*, and when she barked *seas! suigh! ciúnas!* she really meant it. I knew we were in for a dog's life. But even worse was to come: she marched us all in and out of the toilet twice that morning, expecting us all to pee at the same time. To spite her I made up my mind I wouldn't perform — I'd burst first. After lunch she taught us a little poem in Irish. We had to mime flying movements by intertwining our thumbs and moving our fingers in and out while we moved our hands to left and right. We had to recite after her:

> *feidhleachán, feidhleachán,*
> *sciathán dearg, sciathán buí*
> *feidhleachán, feidhleachán.*

This was crap. There was no such thing as a *feidhleachán* with one *sciathán dearg* and the other *buí*, even in Irish, and if each individual *sciathán* was meant to be both *dearg* and *buí* they should have said so. Anyway, all we did with butterflies when we caught them was de-wing them, and little poems in their honour and glory were for little girls.

I soon realised that this was a place for licks, and the fellows from Montenotte were good at that. They brought Miss Byrne little bunches of flowers with silver paper around the stems, and actively participated when she told stories. Like, for instance, when she was explaining the beautiful colours of the cock pheasant, one lad, whose father was a sergeant in the guards, said his father brought one home on Saturday. They were always blowing about the trips they made, like the boy, whose father was a traveller for Barry's Tea, spoofing about going to Charlesfort in Kinsale. They were a fierce crowd of know-alls too, like the one whose mother was a big noise in the Legion of Mary and who claimed that Lourdes water, a bottle of which they were never without at home, was very good for sore throats.

They always got three mixtures for their contributions in class: an acid drop, a bull's eye and a clove rock. I decided that the Lower Road lads were entitled to their share as well, even if we had to bluff to get them. I copped on to the Montenotte fellows and realised that this was like a game of snap. You had to be quick on the draw and in like a flash with 'Miss, miss, my dad brought us there in the summer, miss'.

I got my chance on Friday afternoon during the Irish history lesson. She had gone through the *Book of Invasions* and was as far as the Tuatha Dé Danann. They lived on nectar and salmon and had special magic powers. They planted the hazel woods and built the fairy forts and put crocks of gold at the ends of rainbows. When the Fir Bolg came they gave them a rough time and they had to become leprechauns and go underground. They all wear red pants and green tunics with gold buttons and spend their time having parties, playing music, polishing their gold and mending shoes. You can sometimes hear them in the hedgerows on moonlit nights going tic-tac, tic-tac, tic-tac. If you can catch one and keep your eye on him he'll give you a crock of gold to let him go. But if you take your eye off him for a split second he's gone.

I saw the chance of making a big impression here and says, 'Miss, miss! Waddler and me were looking for birds' nests up the high field one evening when 'twas getting dark and we heard the tic-tac, tic-tac, tic-tac. We poked around and at last found a small fella with a little white beard trying to hide in a furze bush. We put him in a biscuit tin. He said he'd give us the crock of gold he had planked under the rainbow behind Ricey's house if we let him out. We opened the lid a small bit for him to show us exactly where the gold was. He pointed over towards the river. When we looked there was no rainbow, and when we looked back again your man was gone!' I thought Miss Byrne was pleased with my story for she smiled as I told it. When I'd finished all she said was, 'Don't you dare interrupt me during a history lesson again.'

I was dumbfounded. This wasn't fair. The Montenotte boys got mixtures for their stories, and how could she know that mine was made up any more than theirs? I told my father and mother when I got home that the teacher was a right louser and explained why. My dad gave me a penny and I got my mixtures after all.

Miss Byrne began to bug me and I soon concluded that school was only for cissies. Mother had assured me that I'd be reading great stories but the stuff in my school books was crap.

I was fed up, as well, of all the *feidhleachán* and *maidrín-a-rua-rua-rua-rua-rua* shite and made up my own songs. In order to counteract the curriculum crap, I sometimes overstepped the mark. I was so proud of one of my compositions that I taught it to my friends at lunch time and led the recital all the way home in procession behind Miss Byrne:

> *Pounds shillings and pence*
> *The donkey jumped over the fence*
> *He sat on the grass*
> *He tickled his ass*
> *Pounds shillings and pence.*

The more she ignored us the more we shouted. We couldn't understand why she didn't react, and we became more obstreperous consequently, attracting more recruits as we went along. Before she reached home she was like the Pied Piper of Hamelin with half the school in her wake. We were hysterical with laughter as she hurried in home and banged the door. Next day we were hauled before the assembled school and asked if we'd like to sing in as full-throated and fine a voice the song we sang the day before. Our revelries were truly ended and conscience made cowards of us all. She really had us in a spot and she knew it. She lambasted us collectively and individually, saying we were a disgrace to the class and the school, a crowd of good-for-nothing yobos whose parents would even be ashamed of them. We were forced to apologise humbly and were despatched to the headmistress, who kept an ash rod for the chastisement of such serious transgressions.

School became a right pain in the arse after that and I never saw eye to eye with Miss Byrne anymore. Everything she said seemed to me to begin with don't and I always seemed to be asking 'why?' Her stories were all about good little girls who were friendly with everyone, who always helped their hard-working mothers, were sent as maids to cruel landlords, and were finally rescued from the jaws of mad animals by heroes who fell in love with them because of their long golden hair. Miss Byrne knew I was bored.

She never believed me either. One day I had the runs and when I put up my hand and asked, 'An bhfuil cead agam dul amach, más é do thoil é?' she left a shout that only added to my sad condition. A lad who sat in the desk behind me kept prodding my bottom with a ruler, pinching his nose and repeating, 'There's an awful stink, there's an awful stink'. Eventually, when she felt the distraction too much for the rest of the class, she sent me home. Given the state I was in, 'twas a long uncomfortable walk. All the way down Gardiner's Hill and O'Mahony's Avenue I glanced around furtively and, as discreetly as I could, wiped the scutter that ran down the back of my leg with the grease-proof paper in which my lunch had been wrapped. I have never forgotten the indignity of it all.

After first class we were despatched to the boys' school. Things went in five year cycles here and 'twas pot luck as to who you were landed with. There was for, but mostly against, each of the masters, and their legends preceded them. One principal had thrown the school bell at a pupil's father and knocked him out for three hours. That was forty years ago but was still remembered. The second in command specialised in capital punishment. He seasoned a variety of hazel rods up the chimney and soaked them in linseed oil to make them good and heavy. The fat rigid one was for minor transgressions like talking in class, the long thin springy one with the sting for the more serious, like telling someone to fuck off.

Had we a choice of teacher we would have chosen one nicknamed Fluter. He was originally from another county and loved hurling and football. He used to take bus-loads of us to matches in little villages miles away, like Blackrock, Douglas and Bishopstown. The final of the under-twelve city division hurling championship in 1963 was our finest hour, and Fluter spent weeks composing anthems like:

> *Patrick's boys are on the ball,*
> *See them rally to our call,*
> *Make the Mon's poor goalie dance,*
> *Bang them in at every chance.*
> *Steady boys and drive the sliotar*
> *Steady boys and pull together.*
>
> *'Twas on the Mardyke's hurling field*
> *The baffled Mon were forced to yield,*
> *Their mighty hurlers backward reeled*
> *Before the shots of Patrick's boys.*

The Fluter was full of fascinating facts which he shared with us on these hurling expeditions. He told us that throughout history the devil attacked the church in a different way every fifty years. Since 1918 his tactic had been Communism. After 1968 he'd try something else. He also told us that the biggest liner ever built was the *Titanic*. She had been built by the black Protestants in Belfast who said that she was unsinkable. Her number was *NO 9093* and when you held it up against the mirror it read *NO POPE*. And that was why God sank her by putting an iceberg in her way, completely out of the blue, on her maiden voyage.

Our class was very disappointed when we didn't get Fluter. Instead we had Pádraig Ó Duinnín, who expected each of us to be a sort of Gaelic League commando. Even our lunchtime games of 'chasing', 'release', and '1, 2, 3, the book is read' had to be played *as Gaeilge*. It worked, and our class was a kind of élite corps all on its own. We didn't mix with other classes; we developed our own games to suit ourselves, and if any one of our mates was in trouble, we all rallied to his assistance.

Pádraig Ó Duinnín was a *modh díreach* man when it came to teaching. His approach to vocabulary was practical, taking a different topic every week, starting with the familiar and progressing from there. He was a great believer in sensory perception and brought all kinds of props into class so that we could see and feel what he was on about. He brought in models of trains and boats and planes, and not only taught us the words for the various parts, but explained the mechanisms as well. During spring he taught us all about nature and how to identify and distinguish flowers and plants. In autumn we learned to identify trees by their leaves.

One day he brought in a big doll's house and we were going through it step by step, pointing out the various rooms and the different furniture. 'Twas a fairly posh doll's house. We did the main bedroom in detail: 'bedroom = *seomra leapa*'. '*Vardrús* = wardrobe; *bord maisiúchán* = dressing table; *cofrá tarraiceán* = chest of drawers'. Before he left each room he asked, '*Aon rud eile? Aon rud eile anois?*' to make sure we had covered it thoroughly. Remembering that my mother kept the spare linen and the Christmas tablecloth in a tea-chest, I offered 'tea-chest' before we left the bedroom. I was like Archimedes jumping out of his bath shouting 'tea-chest, tea-chest!' and the more the teacher ignored me the more I shouted. Finally he looked at me sympathetically and said, 'ceart go leor, ceart go leor,' and it dawned on me that they didn't keep their clothes in tea-chests in Montenotte. When they were doing the bedclothes I kept my mouth shut, realising that they probably didn't use flour bags as pillowcases in Montenotte either and that their eiderdowns didn't have sleeves like my father's overcoat, which doubled as ours on cold winter nights.

I didn't always put my foot in it and often scored well with an tUasal Ó Duinnín. He was so impressed that he gave me a tanner one day when I reamed off the definition of a right-angled triangle even before we studied it: the square on the hypotenuse is equal to the sum of the squares on the other two sides. I never told my mates that the only reason I knew that was because I'd heard Reilly tell the joke about the Indian woman who had twins lying on a hippopotamus skin, and about whom the Indians said 'the squaw on the hippopotamus is equal to the squaws on the other two hides.' We got on like a house on fire after that. I posted his letters for him on a Friday afternoon in the post office at St Luke's and one Monday morning he picked me out especially to clean the words *f-o-c-k* and *b-a-l-a-x* that had been scribbled on the door at the weekend. I still think of him fondly as the fella Goldsmith had in mind when he wrote:

Beside yon straggling fence that skirts the way,
With blossomed furze unprofitably gay,
There, in his noisy mansion, skill'd to rule,
The village master taught his little school,
A man severe he was and stern to view;

Where We Sported and Played

I knew him well, and every truant knew;
Well had the boding tremblers learned to trace
The day's disasters in his morning face;
Full well they laughed, with counterfeited glee,
At all his jokes, for many a joke had he;
Full well the busy whisper circling round,
Conveyed the dismal tidings when he frowned;
Yet he was kind, or, if severe in aught,
The love he bore to learning was in fault;
The village all declared how much he knew;
'Twas certain he could write and cypher too;
Lands he could measure, terms and tides presage,
And even the story ran that he could gauge.
In arguing too, the parson owned his skill,
For even tho' vanquished, he could argue still;
While words of learned length and thundering sound,
Amazed the gazing rustics ranged around,
And still they gazed, and still the wonder grew,
That one small head could carry all he knew.

(The Deserted Village)

An tUasal Ó Duinnín was a stickler for Christian Doctrine, and we had to learn off by heart fierce intricate definitions of the seven deadly sins and the universality of the Catholic Church. He told us we should be like squirrels building up a hoard of spiritual food to sustain us during our lean adult years. I preferred the straightforward spiritual life of the infant school. There prayer was simple and meaningful: a quickie to the guardian angel in the morning to keep me out of harm's way:

O angel of God, my guardian dear,
To whom God's love commits me here,
Ever this day be at my side
To light and guard, to rule and guide.

Then an all-embracing 'thank you' at school:

Thank you God for the food we eat,
Thank you God for the birds that sing,
Thank you God for everything.

And a God bless everybody and anybody, including the cat and the dog, going to bed.

All that type of prayer was lovely and simple and did the job fine for First Communion. But all the Confirmation stuff about prayer being a raising of the mind and heart to God was much too theoretical for us, and all the talk about the valley of tears gave us a fit of the blues. Then there were big funny-sounding words that were no good in conversation or in essays, like 'compunction', 'restitution', 'beatitudes'. There was spiritual baggage we had to carry with us and work on daily called 'prudence, justice, fortitude and temperance', and things to be avoided like the plague were 'pride, covetousness, lust, anger, gluttony, envy and sloth'.

All this straight-jacket stuff took the kick out of life and I hadn't much time for it. I knew that St Anthony and myself understood each other and I decided to stick with him. He was a dead cert. All you had to do was say three Hail Marys and he came up trumps. The only condition was that you had to concentrate on every word and if your mind wandered for a split second he wouldn't deliver because, in that case, you were not giving him your undivided attention, but really only thinking about yourself. Over a six month period myself and St Anthony were on a roll and he saved my bacon on three impossible occasions: when I lost my father's penknife in the undergrowth in 'The Haunted' and Reilly's dog sniffed it out; when John's sponge ball, which I hit into the river, miraculously got stuck in the piles at low tide; and, my maths exercise copy book that some shagger stole on the way to school on Monday morning was staring me in the face at the foot of Grattan's Hill on my way home in the afternoon.

I was so well in with St Anthony at this stage that I decided to go for the jackpot. I planned to stay awake all night in silent prayer to beseech and implore him to pull a Santa Claus stroke in the middle of summer and place an air gun, which were all the rage at the time, at the foot of my bed. I had seen Moses do spectacular things in *The Ten Commandments* on Saturday in the Palace, like striking the rock and bringing forth water and turning a stick into a snake — and he wasn't even a saint. Delivery on such a simple request as an air gun should be a cinch to St Anthony after that. Unfortunately I fell asleep and never got to test the strength of my faith. I know St Anthony was sorry for me. It must have been hard for him, and we getting on so well lately and all, up there in Heaven with the gun in his hand, ready to give two angels the word to fly down with it, and then having to put it back in the store and leave it there till Christmas probably.

A week later I borrowed an air gun, unknown to my parents, but had no luck with it. In the quarry my sister Alice dared me to fire at her and I did. I hit her just below the knee. She had to be brought to the North Infirmary to have the pellet removed and got four stitches. I tried to hide the air gun behind the tea-chest on the landing at the top of the stairs but, in my haste, I knocked over and broke the head off the statue of the Infant of Prague. I tried to hide the broken bits under the tea-chest but 'twas no good: my mother went looking for him on the Friday night to ensure a fine day for my Confirmation on the Saturday. When it lashed out of the heavens she said it was the Infant of Prague getting his own back on me.

Shortly afterwards I redeemed myself in my parents' eyes by winning a Gaeltacht scholarship to Ballingeary. On one of his regular Saturday night visits my uncle Denis mentioned that the GAA were awarding scholarships that summer and that oral examinations would be held in the Gaelic League Headquarters, the Áras, the following week. He told my parents to make sure that I was there. When my uncle Denis spoke, the case was closed. I wasn't too enthusiastic about going to a corny country place to speak Irish for the whole month of July, but my mother's mind was made up. 'Sure aren't you a great Ireeshion!' she said and that was that.

The oral exam itself was a cake-walk. I was asked a whole lot of stupid questions about the best book I ever read, my pet aversion, and why I wanted to go to the Gaeltacht. To the first I answered that I wasn't much into books but that I thought *The Boy's Own* was brilliant and that *Taidhgín Tréan an Leanbh Láidir* was the best story I had ever read. As regards the second, I said that as a Christian I really didn't have a pet aversion but that there were things I didn't like and people I wasn't very fond of but that I really didn't hate them like I hated porridge or the English. I had to bullshit my way through the last and said that in Ballingeary they spoke our native tongue; 'twas one of the few places where Gael and Gaeilge had never been subdued; the spirit of 1916 still lived there and we should all repair there to drink from that well and rekindle the flame. I thought that was a brilliant answer. They did too and gave me one of the scholarships.

We went in single decker buses from the bus station in Parnell Place on Saturday morning. I didn't want to go at all and nearly funked it at breakfast time. I always got sick in the bus and was about to use that as an excuse, but when I looked at my father and mother I could see they were fierce proud of me, and for once I couldn't bring myself to disappoint them. My father asked me if I had enough money, and when I said 'I have, thanks', in a nervous sort of way, he gave me another pound and said, 'Look after yourself down there now, do ye hear me, and stay out of harm's way.'

'OK,' I said, and he went off to work.

Where We Sported and Played

Mother came with me to the bus station. I could see that my being as good as the snobby crowd that were going gave her great satisfaction. The lads were nearly all from Presentation or Christian College, the girls from St Als and Ardfoyle. Their fathers had driven them to the bus that morning but I didn't give a shite. You'd think they were emigrating to Australia, never to be seen again, with all the commotion. Just before the bus left all the parents came on to make sure that everything was all right. My mother was as good as the rest of them, and on she came to remind me again to be sure to be careful when swimming and cycling. Unlike the rest of the whinging parents I noticed she had a quiet contented smile. She knew that I was half-way up the social ladder already and that if I could make it here I'd make it anywhere.

When we arrived in Ballingeary there was a mad scamper into the hostel. It was too late when I realised that those who had been there before knew the score and picked the best beds. I had to make do with the worst one in the house. It was a big open dormitory with thirty-six beds: fifteen along each wall and six in a line down the middle between them. The first in that line was all that was left for me, in full view of all the lads and the teacher in charge.

As regards Irish, Ballingeary was crap. Few spoke it and the teachers weren't going to break their balls for an ideal. We had compulsory language class in the morning, which was an awful bore. Twice a week a *cigire* went around with a basket of sweets in a effort to encourage competition. I won a packet of silvermints for knowing the Irish for a jet (*scaird eitealán*) and a packet of Toffos for a flea (*dreancaide*).

The song and dance teacher was a big, fat, flabby lump of a man. With his *Beidh Aonach Amárach i gContae an Chláir, Bhíos-sa Lá i bPhortláirge,* and *Trasna na dTonnta,* he was fighting a losing battle against Elvis and the Everly brothers as far as we were concerned. The dancing was even worse than the singing. He sweated his way through his *aon, dó, trís* with his big belly swinging. I felt a right fool doing these silly steps and dreaded to think what my hardchaw friends on the Lower Road would say if they could have seen me now. Some holiday camp this where you'd be sent home if caught smoking and where girls were forbidden to wear slacks, even when mountain climbing.

I'd never have stuck it at all if it wasn't for the *craic* at the *céilí* every night. Some of the women were right lashers. We spent a lot of time dollying ourselves up every night in anticipation of the big move: washing, combing, cleaning teeth, polishing shoes. All that nearly took as long as the *céilí* itself which lasted from 8.00pm to 10.00pm.

We were all lined up at one side of the hall, the girls on the other. The first few days 'twas a free-for-all, with both sides sizing each other up and drawing up mental lists of preferences. As the days progressed things settled down somewhat, and we realised that somehow the lists of preferences drawn up in the privacy of our own minds were remarkably similar, which meant that if you put your eye on somebody you had to be fairly quick off the mark because the minute the dance was announced there was a stampede across the floor. Timing was of the essence: if you were too slow you missed your chance; too fast and you frightened them away. Lady's choice was one dance a night you just had to play by ear. It didn't pay to be too much of a Casanova standing in front with your chest sticking out and your hands in your pockets with all the bravado of a cock on a dung heap. That frightened them away as well. But if the understanding was there and a girl really interested and you positioned yourself round about middle of the crowd, she'd find you all right.

Particular friendships were frowned upon and you had

to be discreet about your business. I had my eye on a girl called Ursula and thought of a way to crack the system. I let the first few dances go before making my move: *Fallaí Luimní* and *Ionsaí na hInse* were no good because you were on the move all the time and didn't get a chance to chat a girl up. The *Cor Beirte* was your man. Here you were with the same girl all the time, waltzing and swinging. The first chance I got I made my move and asked Ursula if she'd go for a spin on the bike to Guagán Barra next day. She said she'd see. I liked that. It meant that she was no daw. She asked me out for lady's choice and I knew then that I was away on a hack. The only snag was that the dance was *Baint an Fhéir* and we had no chance to talk, except during one of the swings when she said 'OK,' and Guagán Barra was on. After *Amhrán na bhFiann* there was a mad rush to the exit where two teacher supervised us strictly to ensure that we went back to the dormitory in the same company that we came to the hall in. I timed my push so as to be close to Ursula. Under the watchful eye of the teacher you couldn't do much, but I gave her a quick wink and was thrilled when she winked back.

All next morning I was very excited and couldn't eat my dinner at all. Half-way to Guagán Barra I stopped to wait for Ursula. I sat down on the grass margin for a smoke and inhaled deeply, more out of nervousness than pleasure. 'Twas a beautiful day and, as I lay there looking up at the clear blue sky, I heard a horse neigh and a corncrake croak continually with satisfaction. He was still croaking an hour later, but there was no Ursula and he began to bug me. I smoked another fag nervously and, half an hour later, even the crickets began to bug me. She had given me a fifty and I didn't know how to handle it. If a fella led you up the garden path you could fuck him out of it or give him a dig. 'Twas different with girls and I didn't know what to do, but one thing was certain: I was finished with the blonde from Blackrock.

Where We Sported and Played

I got my own back on her that night at the *céilí* and ignored her. When she asked me out for lady's choice I knew it wasn't polite to refuse so I consented, but I was very cool to her. When she said she was sorry she couldn't make it that afternoon I just shook my head and grunted 'ugh!' as much as to say "tis all the one to me'. But then she told me she got a puncture and I felt a right eejit for being mad at her. I was delighted that there was a reasonable explanation for something I knew would have been completely out of character for her.

On the last night, when the teachers were otherwise engaged, I walked her home and she let me hold her hand. I felt most uncomfortable. I didn't know whether I should swing along with her hand in mine, or squeeze it, or what. I knew she was in the same dilemma. So I just kept my hand stiff and it sweated. The more I thought about it and wished it to stop the more it sweated. It must have felt like a dead fish. When we finally reached the house where she was staying I nuzzled up to kiss her goodnight, but I wasn't very successful at that either and my nose began to run. She gave me a passport photograph and we promised to meet in Cork, but some bastard stole it on the bus home next day and I never saw Ursula again. Still, first impressions last, and whenever a *fear an tí* at a *céilí* announces *An Cor Beirte* I'm a thirteen year old in Ballingeary all over again.

My mother was right when she said that the trip to Ballingeary would either make or break me. I came perilously close to the latter, and was lucky I wasn't expelled after a visit to a recreation park in Inchigeela that got out of hand. Four of us went there one free afternoon. We hired some clubs and played pitch and putt, none too successfully, leaving pock marks on the greens and disturbing a leisurely crowd of English visitors by running across their paths, applauding good shots and cursing bad ones, bending down to implore and coax balls into holes, and fucking them when they didn't. They said we were a bunch of hooligans who shouldn't be allowed to play there, and we replied by telling them that we were more entitled to be there than the bloody Brits. Because we hadn't much of a clue, the novelty of the game soon wore off and, when I saw a punt moored to a tree on the bank, I suggested we try the river. We had no oars but that didn't matter; we let her drift with the current, not concerned where we'd end up. I was delighted to show off my expertise on the river. My friends were thrilled and they marvelled at my skill. We shouted and roared with delight as we splashed and rolled along.

A teacher from a nearby college saw us and made a formal complaint to the headmaster in Ballingeary. After tea we were called to his office to be disciplined. He banged the table in anger and scared the shite out of us. One of the lads from Presentation College who fancied himself as an Ireeshion said to leave the talking to him. He made a right balls of it. Instead of having the cop to eat humble pie and apologise profusely, he kept saying 'ach ... ach... ach' by way of explanation to all of his rhetorical questions: 'Don't you know the river is out of bounds? Who gave you permission? What do you think this college is, Butlins?' He said that this was no minor matter and that he'd have to take a very serious view of it, that he would have no hesitation in sending us home but for the fact that our record at speaking Irish was so good, and instead he would impose a fine of half-crown on each of us. I felt terribly aggrieved when he took my last half-crown, and was determined to get even. I got my chance at the week-end.

In an effort to encourage tidiness and order there were domestic competitions every Saturday, one for the group with the best-kept dormitory and one for the individual with the best-dressed bed. The group prize was a box of sweets, the individual one ten shillings. I was broke and decided to go all out for the ten shillings. The new tubular beds with their foam mattresses were easy to make look good. Mine was a big old iron bed with a horsehair mattress that sagged in the middle. I turned this handicap into an advantage and put in a special effort to bring it up to scratch: I tightened the springs with bits of a coat hanger, turned the mattress, cleaned the frame with a damp cloth and paid particular attention to tucking in the bedclothes so that if someone bent down and inspected them from underneath he'd see that they were neatly pleated and dovetailed together. I brushed not only the immediate area of my own bed but six foot on either side as well and arranged my two cases parallel to one another to head and foot.

The inspection was carried out on Saturday afternoon and the winners were announced after breakfast on Sunday morning. The headmaster was in his element when calling out the winners. Our dormitory didn't win the box of sweets but I can still hear his voice, with all the ceremony he could muster, announce the individual winner: 'An chéad leaba i lár baill sa seomra fada'. I couldn't believe it. Somebody up there liked me after all. I had been vindicated, and I walked up proudly to collect my ten bob note. He couldn't believe it either. All he could ask was, 'an bhfuil tú cinnte gur tusa atá i gceist?' But sure I was sure and he knew that the look of satisfaction and serenity on my face said it all.

4

WORK

Because we never had much, and pocket money was unheard of, we were always on the look-out for a few bob. Before I went to school I could never understand how my father could pass a sweet shop while loose change jingled in his pocket. By the time I was six I realised that money didn't grow on trees, and that I'd have to work for what I'd get. During winter we sold bundles of kindling from door to door made from old (and sometimes new) pallets, butter and orange boxes we fished out of the river. We chopped and arranged it in neat little bundles held together by elastic rings cut from an old bicycle tube. They sold for a penny a bundle, which was cheap, but then, sometimes the wood wasn't too dry.

Supply didn't always match demand. One particularly cold winter there was at least £1 to be made every Saturday but we couldn't get enough timber. On Friday afternoon as I scanned the river, one of the huge piles used to support the quay wall, 2' square by 40' long, floated into my ken. 'Never look a gift horse in the mouth,' says I, and 'where there's a will there's a way'. I told Waddler to hold on to the rope while I bent over the quay wall to put a lasso around this beauty. Waddler said I was mad and that we'd never be able to make kindling out of a yoke like that. 'First things first,' says I, 'we'll worry about that when we'll get her in'. With the lasso secure we eased her nice and gently with the current, along the quay wall towards the slip. But when we got her around the corner she was too heavy to haul in. I could see 5,000 bundles of kindling, which translated into 5,000 pennies, hanging in the balance, and I wasn't going to give in that easily. I edged out along the wall between slip and river and tugged furiously at the rope. 'Come on ye bitch!' Bang! The rope broke and down I went into four foot of dirty oily water full of flotsam and jetsam. When I got home my mother lost the rag with me altogether. She stripped me in the kitchen and made me stand there starkers while all the children on the lane ran in and out of our hall and had a good gawk and a giggle, as though they were at the circus. I was mortified, but my mother had her mind made up to teach me a lesson. I stayed away from the river for a while after that.

We made some easy money at Christmas time, short and seasonal and all as it was, and over the years must have stripped hundreds of holly trees in Tivoli and Montenotte. We raided after dark and people got really mad next morning, I imagine, when they saw their beautiful trees, so carefully pruned and trained, horribly mutilated or missing altogether, and their gardens and avenues ruined. Four days before Christmas we cut the holly up and tied it in neat bunches, tying every two together and suspending them over a long pole which Waddler and Murphy carried on their shoulders, while I did the trading at the doors: 6d. for a bunch of the ordinary red berry, 9d. for the variegated. We sold until 5 o'clock on Christmas eve and then went off to sing Christmas carols at the opening of the crib.

On St Stephen's Day we made a few bob as well by going around with the wren and waking people up at an unmerciful hour of the morning. We didn't dress up and had no wren, musical instruments or dancers or anything. Just a bit of holly and a song that carried a threat:

The wren, the wren
The king of all birds,
St Stephen's Day got caught in the furze,
Up with the kettles and down with the pots,
Give us our answer and let us be off.

Where We Sported and Played

As I went up the Lower Road,
I saw a bird on top of a wall.
Up with me stick and I gave him a fall
And brought him here to visit ye all.

God bless the mistress of this house,
A golden chain around her neck,
If she's sick or if she's sore
The Lord have mercy on her soul.

Knock at the knocker, ring at the bell,
Give us our answer for singing so well,
Singing so well, singing so well....

And we kept that up until someone answered. Most people were quick to give us a few pence because they had a lingering suspicion that 'twould bring them bad luck if they didn't, and were delighted to get rid of us. One woman in Myrtle Hill used to wait in the hall till we had finished and always gave us a tanner when we sang the second last verse for her again. We went to the pictures after dinner and, as my grandmother was my godmother as well, I bought her a pint bottle of Murphy's stout as a Christmas present on the way home.

Once, when I was desperate for a few bob, I sold a make-shift bike for five shillings. It was fairly basic: a heavy Rudge frame, a hard racing saddle, dropped handlebars and a lethal fix-wheel. It had no brakes or mudguards. It had once been a fully-endowed Rudge, but had lain discarded for years in Hyde's outhouse since the cog-wheel broke, and various parts had been removed periodically as they were needed to repair other machines. I fixed the wheel by removing the casing and jamming a small nut in the cog. You could pedal like the devil now but you couldn't free-wheel. Murphy wasn't to know that when he bought the contraption, and nearly broke his neck careering down O'Mahony's Avenue when his leg got stuck between the pedal and the frame. I had to give him back his five bob and go back to the drawing-board.

Alterations demanded the removal of the back wheel, but all the threads were damaged and I couldn't loosen the nuts. It was just around the corner of the lane and I was lashing into it with a hammer, in my annoyance using my most potent bad language: 'fecking bitch, fecking bitch...' as though it were a working shanty like 'Ding Dong Dedero'. A neighbour got the shock of her life when she came around the corner and heard the music. She ran straight into the hall to my mother shouting, 'Jesus, Mary and Joseph! D'ya hear the language out a him outside there?' This was so serious that my mother said she'd wait for my father to come home from work to deal with me. 'You'll have to put your foot down with that fella now, Leo,' she said.

'That's the end of your gallivantin' now, me boy, with bikes,' he said. 'I won't be long putting a stop to your gallop'.

Next morning my mother told me that they had decided to send me to be an altar boy. Colm Brown had just retired from the altar and she bought his red soutane and white surplice for five shillings. The Latin and the rubrics were no bother to me and I picked them up in a week. But I had some difficulty adjusting to the work ethic and the reality of the shop floor. The carry-on behind the scenes was just like that in a theatre: the priests talked out loud about sport and the news and everything in the sacristy, and even smoked in the room upstairs. Behind the altar were all kinds of props and stools and stands which you never saw when you were at mass. The racks of penny candles had to be counted, emptied and replaced. All of this had a disturbing effect on me. I felt cheated, just as I had when I found out that adults were only fooling us about Christmas, and that Santa Claus was only *mar dhea*. The

74

magic and the mystery of Christmas died with the Santa Claus myth, and the horrific thought that God was the same was too shocking to contemplate. But a priest explained to me that God works through people, and eventually I got over the shock.

Then I realised that God helps those who help themselves and that there were business opportunities here too: you'd get 2s.6d. or five shillings, if you were lucky, for serving at a wedding. The senior altar boys had a monopoly on the trade and weddings went in strict order of seniority. I decided that the only way around this was to lick up to the sacristan. I arrived before the others in the morning to help him prepare the altar, cleaned up for him when mass was finished and ran the errands that he was supposed to be running for the priests. It worked, and I was soon in on the big time. Then I wanted a bigger slice of the action and volunteered to serve early morning mass all through Lent. This worked so well that he gave me five weddings during Easter week and I made a fortune. My fellow servers were bucking and decided that they'd have to put a stop to this. After Benediction on the Sunday they cornered me in the sacristy. I didn't take kindly to being pushed around by a senior altar boy. Canon Bastible came in and caught us fighting in full regalia. He fired both of us on the spot. I had served for nine months at this stage which was a respectable enough stretch, and was able to convince most people that I was moving aside so that some more young lads would get their chance.

Almost everybody trusted altar boys and 'twas that impeccable reference that landed a big job for Waddler and myself when the two old Spencer sisters, to whom we sold kindling regularly, offered us £3 to paint the kitchen. We told them we'd start at 9 o'clock on Saturday morning and gave them a list of what was needed: a gallon of Snocem for the walls, two pints of white gloss for the skirting and door, and a bottle of turpentine. They needn't bother with scrapers and brushes — we'd bring them ourselves. After a brief inspection on the Saturday morning we told them that the table and chairs, the curtains and the picture of the Sacred Heart would have to be removed. The dresser was too heavy but no matter, we could work around it, and the Turkish carpet, which was jammed in under the skirting, could be covered with two old sheets.

We flew through the ceiling and walls with the big distemper brush and had them finished by 12 o'clock. The two ould wans were delighted and fierce excited, running in and out all the time to see how we were getting on. They gave us tea and biscuits before we started the gloss work. I told them in no uncertain terms that this was slow work on which we would have to concentrate, working delicately along the skirting, and not to be coming in and out all the time distracting us. We started off under the far window, one of us on the left, the other on the right, and worked away along both sides towards the front to meet at the door. That would leave only the outside of the door and frame to be completed.

Waddler was so excited when we reached the door that he forgot I was coming from the other side, and he got up so quickly that he kicked over my tin of paint. Out it flowed through the joining where the two sheets met and onto the lovely Turkish carpet. 'Go away, ye gowl,' says I, 'now we're rightly up shit creek', and I could see the £3 disappear before my very eyes. I looked around in panic and saw a cat perched outside on the window sill. 'Leave in that cat and keep a good hold of her,' says I, grabbing a cloth and soaking it in turpentine. I gave her a good dabbing on the arse and said, 'you can leave her go now,' and she freaked around the room, dragging the spilled paint all over the place.

I opened the door gently and, after a few seconds, shouted, 'Who let in that cat? She's after destroying the place on us!' The sisters came running and, when they saw the state of the place, started arguing among themselves. I said 'twas no good crying over spilled milk and that if they got another bottle of turpentine and a few cloths we'd do our best to clean up the mess. When we were finished, the carpet looked better than it had for years, with a deep wine colour and a lovely fresh smell. The sisters were so delighted that they gave us more tea and biscuits and £1 extra.

That was 1962 and about the same time we went into the scrap metal business. The Fisheries weren't exactly the mighty Yukon but the mud flats where the boats were mended was our Klondike. Copper fetched a shilling a pound, brass and lead 4 pence, and that was gold to us. We could always be seen at ebb tide, as assiduous as any turnstone, fishing for old copper nails, brass screws and lead weights, until our gallon paint tins were eventually filled. Most of us preferred to work in steady partnerships of two than in the bigger syndicate of the gang. This meant we needed little organisation and no hierarchical structure, and it even afforded us a chance of raiding off the gangs occasionally.

Irish Steel was set up in Cork Harbour in 1947, and Cork became the Mecca of all the scrap dealers in the country. Lorry-loads of scrap were piled on the quayside at Water Street for shipment downstream by barge once a week. A scrap mountain like this was a knacker's paradise and it was necessary to provide a watchman to protect it, lest some of them decided to recycle it in their own way by selling it back again to the merchants who sold it to Irish Steel. Strictly speaking it was unlawful for us to tinker with any of it as well, but our pilfering was regarded as innocent, if annoying, and as harmless as that of pigeons at a grain store. At times the place resembled a gigantic ant hill as we crawled up precarious girders or lay dangerously under old Thames Trader engines, painstakingly removing old brass and copper screws, or frantically hammering at old cast-iron cisterns in order to remove the precious copper ballcocks.

In time we progressed to even more intricate removals. A Kerry immigrant, later to become a friend of mine, whose father worked on the railway and had recently been transferred to Cork, once remarked that we would make a fortune if we could devise a means of removing the copper from the starter motors which still remained attached to the scrapped engines. Reluctant as my Kerry friend was to admit it, he pronounced that it couldn't be done, and he allowed us to tinker with the dynamo he had removed and which bore the marks of his despairing efforts in the bruised copper.

I was something of an experimental chemist at the time and never ceased to be amazed at the marvellous purifying properties of fire. As an experiment, the watchman kindly allowed us to place a dynamo in his fire brazier, and when it was cool and the carbon insulation burned away, Eureka! The copper was easily picked out with a screw-driver. We were in the big time now! This was the great copper rush, but it had a consequent waste disposal problem. We had to hide the iron skeleton of the dynamo denuded of the copper, lest our Kerry friend realise that where there's a will there's a way, and we expertly packed them away in the old cisterns from which we had already removed the ballcocks, under old wheel bellows and cast-iron stoves.

Sometimes the stuff wasn't so accessible, having fallen from the huge magnet into the river when being transferred from quayside to barge. At low tide a whole array of starter motors full of copper fuel pipes and brass gearbox keys could be seen embedded in the mud. One lean Friday afternoon I found the sight irresistible, racked my brains to find a way to retrieve the hoard from the slob, and in the end decided to risk it, on the assumption that if I could get down I'd be able to get back up again. I slithered down the quay wall and plonked into the mud. I knew what Howard Carter must have felt like when he stumbled on Tutankhamen's tomb and, as greed got the better of me, I completely lost the run of myself. I wrenched everything I could from the mud and threw it up onto the quayside.

But I stayed too long, and was trapped by the incoming tide and forced towards the highest part of the quay wall. I tried everything: climbing, but the film of waste oil which coated the wall made it impossible; running and jumping, but couldn't build up speed because of the mud; poking bits of metal into the fissures between the limestone blocks to form a ladder, but 'twas no good. I had to admit defeat and the tide was coming in fast. 'Help! Help!' I shouted, but nobody in Barry's timber yard or the railway, although I was immediately beneath them on their side of the river, heard me. My voice carried across the surface of the river and all the workers in Ford and Dunlop on the other side came out. They drew the attention of the Harbour Commissioners who came to get me in their launch.

In time we became something of scrap merchants ourselves. Whenever we sensed that a house was about to be converted from gas to what was the more fashionable electricity in those days, we were on hand to tender for the lead. Most people were delighted to be relieved of it, and gave it to us for free when they found that we provided free removal in our own box-car: the weighty lead as ballast across the axle; the copper and brass to forehead and aft; and over the top, the occasional horse-hair mattress, which we were somewhat adverse to taking because of its awkward bulkiness and connotations of dire poverty.

We became so obsessed with filling the box-car that sometimes we overstepped the mark. When a local pub was sold we moved in before the new owners and had the joint cleaned out: a big copper draining-board and wash basin, all the lead piping and brass fittings. Water squirted everywhere before we succeeded in plugging the main, and there was a ferocious smell of gas when we wrenched the meter out. We got so much stuff we had to take it out in six old bottle crates.

Saturday morning was fair day and we rolled off up the Lower Road and the Quays to the small scrap dealers who inhabited what remained of Jew Town in Douglas Street and Victoria Road, and in front of the grand edifice of Cork's synagogue we sold our hoard. Our names and addresses were always requested, for this was a dicey trade, and some shady characters were flogging merchandise that wasn't always scrap.

Waddler nearly blew it on us one day when we arrived at the dealers. Someone had stolen a load of telephone cable and a detective was in the office checking the list. He sized us up through the window while our stuff was being weighed. While all of it wasn't strictly legitimate, we had no telephone cable, and I told Waddler to hold tight and we'd bluff our way out of this one. But 'twas no good. The detective came out of the office quickly with a grin on his face. Waddler began to whimper.

'Is he all right?' asked the detective.

'Arah, he's flayed out after dragging that ould stuff me grandmother gave us all the way up from the Lower Road, but he'll be all right in a minute,' I said.

He gave Waddler an affectionate pat on the head and was gone, having found his man on the list in the office. 'Twas the closest shave I ever had.

We regarded ten bob each as a satisfactory reward for our week's work. If we didn't make the pound between us we were usually a bit despondent. A pound meant the Coliseum or the Capitol and an afternoon of *Laurel and Hardy*, *Tarzan*, *The Three Stooges*, *Al Capone* and the fascinating sequences of *Movietone News* about the latest in the Royal Air Force or the big fight game in America. We stared in goggle-eyed stupefaction as we gorged ourselves on popcorn and ice-cream, and chain-smoked Woodbines in the privacy of the stalls. Anything less than a pound meant the

Where We Sported and Played

Assembs — the grand Assembly Rooms of old — now not so grand as the gurriers of the Marsh and Rocksavage engaged in running battles up and down the aisles and came between us, the screen, and any possible suspension of disbelief.

We'd come home at tea time feeling as fed up as the fellow in the parable of the talents who blew it. Had we had sense we could have doubled the little we had in a fortnight and eventually owned a bike. But we had no sense. After tea we were ordered off to confession where we were shriven of the sins of the week: the greed and covetousness that ruled our scrap-collecting, the gluttony of the Saturday afternoon, and the ensuing despair. Sunday was a day of rest and recreation and on Mondays we were on the job again.

I got my first summer job in Silver Springs Hotel in 1964. I worked like a slave in the staff canteen from 8 o'clock in the morning till 12 noon, and from 3.00pm to 6.00pm seven days a week, with every second Sunday off, for £2.20 a week. I was expected to prepare the dining area, dance attendance on and clean up after all the waitresses, porters and kitchen staff. One day when taking a sixth consecutive tray of their dirty ware to the wash-up some of it fell and broke. The wash-up from the dining-room the night before had been piled high on the counter. I plonked my own stuff on top of it because there was nowhere else to put it. The fella on the wash-up machine didn't come to work that day. It wasn't my fault when the lot came tumbling down. 'Go 'way, ye feckin' eejit!' one of the chefs shouted, 'you should be made pay for it out of your wages'. I had had enough of this hell after three weeks: 'Shag off out of that, ye fat fecker, it wasn't my fault. Anyway, if I had to pay 'twould take me two months, with the lousy money I get for dancing attendance on a shower of shites like you.' I ran off and never went back there again.

I was happy that I'd stood up for myself and not let

anybody walk on me, but was a bit annoyed that I'd lasted only three weeks, and a long empty-handed summer facing me. I was on the look-out for another job and at the gang meeting on Saturday morning I got my chance. I overheard Reilly tell the lads that Michael O'Brien, the butcher, had asked him to come out to his farm that afternoon to give a hand, but that he got plenty of pocket money from his brothers and wasn't really interested. I tore off up the road to the butcher's and said, 'Reilly sent me up to say he can't come to work for you today.' I was sure he'd say, 'Sugar, now I'm rightly stuck. Would you come yourself?' But he didn't. 'Is that all right so?' says I, kinda panicky, when I saw my job slipping away from me. He said nothing and, having stood there for a while doing nothing, I had to leave. I was mad at myself for funking it, for trying to be devious, instead of coming straight out with the question, or saying something like 'If you want some help, I'm your man.'

I psyched myself up for a week and on the following Saturday came straight to the point. He was just about to say 'no' when his wife nudged him and said, 'We'll give you five shillings for doing deliveries and cleaning the place from 9.00am till 7.00pm. Is that all right?'

'Grand,' I said.

I delivered the Sunday roast to twenty houses in Montenotte. They tipped me with sweets and fruit. I made the dinner for himself and herself and myself and got two cream buns with the cup of tea afterwards — a treat for which I'd almost have worked for nothing. Before finishing I brushed, washed and freshly saw-dusted the floor.

For a full year I spent the five shillings on the weekly parts of the encyclopaedias *Mind Alive* and *History of the 20th Century* and began to educate myself. I had a lot of ground to make up as regards vocabulary, and waded tediously through a 1920s edition of *Cassells Dictionary* which I had on more or less permanent loan from the Railway Dormitory library. I marked all the words I didn't understand and arranged them in groups. I had a weakness for Italian and exotic-sounding ones like *fiasco, manifesto, taboo, pariah, putschists* which would add colour to any essay. Big Greek and Latin ones sounded learned and scientific: *archetypal, anathema, xenophobic, pharmacopoeia, pragmatic, iconoclastic, desultory, intransigent, ephemeral, indigenous.* A mastery of prefixes like *neo-, pseudo-, quasi-,* and *ultra-,* meant you could really lay it on, or refine any statement as you wished.

I beefed up on knowledge as well and divided my memory into two dramatic categories: one of leaders—Lawrence of Arabia, Pádraig Pearse, Ataturk, Mussolini, Franco, Roosevelt, Stalin, De Gaulle, De Valera, Kennedy, Khruschev, Mao, Perón, Che Guevara. The other category was one of battles: the Dardanelles, Jutland, Verdun, the Somme, Pearl Harbour, El Alamein, Stalingrad, D-Day. *Mind Alive* had fascinating articles under a wide range of headings, which included *Arts,* with catchy titles like 'In the Footsteps of Homer' and 'Music for the Millions'. The geography section took me on a grand tour 'Exploring the Earth's Hidden Depths', 'Where Man lives and Why', 'Life in the City'. The section on 'Man and Medicine' brought me right inside a hospital and explained all about the nervous system. I became something of a philosopher under the influence of the section called *Ideas,* questioning concepts like 'What is a Gentleman?' and expounding eloquently on 'The Right to Freedom' and 'The Nature of Knowledge'. And so, in a pre-television age, I travelled and analysed the world with my own imagination and at my own pace.

All seasons had their compensations. Christmas was hardly over when we began to turn our minds to other sources of revenue. We treated birds' eggs as currency and valued them according to rarity: a swan's, £1; the duck family, sea-gull's and wood-cock's, 10s.; crow's 2s.6d., pigeon's and skylark's, 1s.; wagtail's, thrush's, wren's, sparrow's, robin's, 6d.; and 3d. for a blackbird's because any eejit could find a blackbird's nest.

When I was coming from a funeral in St Finbarr's one day with my father, I saw a swan's nest on a tiny little island in the Lee where it flows through the university. This was miles away from base camp but I decided 'twas worth a bash. On Saturday morning Waddler and I took the bus to town. We told our parents that we were studying the Civil War in school and were going up Fitzgerald's Park to see Michael Collins' uniform in the museum. The nest was only a stone's throw from there. The high wall and the trees gave us great cover from the road and we could only be seen from the top of a double-decker bus.

I climbed out along a pole to the island with a big stick in my hand. The cob stood up and hissed at me but I gave him a few wallops of the stick and he funked it and went off into the river. But there was no budging your wan on the nest. She stood up and hissed and flapped her wings and no amount of lashing would move her. She made a go for me a few times and I was beginning to have second thoughts about the value of a swan's egg. I knew that one belt of her wing would break my arm. "Tis no good,' says I, 'the bitch won't budge. There's only one thing for it: we'll have to get a rope. 'Tis too far to go back home. We'll have to hobble a clothes line somewhere.'

On the Western Road 'twas only a matter of taking your pick. There was nothing but big back gardens with clothes lines everywhere. Out I climbed again and tried to lasso your wan on the nest. Waddler held the far end and I threw the noose but she had her neck bent like a coat hanger, ready to peck me, and the ring was too small to go around her. I made a huge circle this time and as she flapped the noose caught her around the neck and wing. Waddler pulled, the noose tightened, and out she came as easy as a chicken. I grabbed the eggs and shot back to the bank. When Waddler let go the rope the noose slackened, she flapped her wings, the lasso fell off and there wasn't a bother on her.

An ould fella upstairs in a bus saw us and got all annoyed, banging the window and shaking his fist and everything. But he wasn't concerned enough about the swan to get off the bus there and then to catch us. However, just in case he might report us when he got into town, we skidaddled off fast towards the museum, across the North Gate Bridge and down Pope's Quay miles away. Waddler was fierce disappointed. There were only two eggs in the nest. One was a beauty, a heavy, solid lime-green ball the size of a big chocolate Easter egg; the other a small little *gliogar* like a hen's egg. I gave him the *gliogar*.

When we got home I got a hammer, a 4-inch nail and an empty paint tin. I hammered two holes at opposite ends of the shell and blew the egg into the tin. Then I tossed it from hand to hand in wonder and admiration, like the head-hunters in Papua, New Guinea. While I was doing all this Waddler was trying to bribe me to part with it. He offered me his brother's penknife, hurley and sponge ball. No way. Then he offered me two sixty-four pagers. I said 'no'.

'Right,' he said, 'I'll give ya the penknife, the sponger, the "64s", the *Beezers* and all his *Hotspurs* and *Victors*'.'

I couldn't resist that and said, 'all right, but you'll have to give them all to me now'. He did.

Before I had them packed away under my bed I knew that I had made a mistake. The penknife was rusty, the sponger was frayed, the cover was missing off one of the '64s', and the other had only fifty pages. I didn't fancy *The Hotspur* or *The Victor* either. I wasn't into soccer and they were all full of Roy of the Rovers stuff, or else British soldiers who were all heroes fighting against unbelievable odds, always responding bravely and willingly to commands like 'up an' at 'em, lads,' and were awarded the

Where We Sported and Played

Victoria Cross for killing German soldiers called 'Hans'.

I couldn't be bothered wasting my time with that kind of rubbish and instead of that used to sneak odd copies of *Hobbies Weekly* out of the bottom of the big black box in which my father kept his tools. This belonged to the real world, the editorial comment very often like an encouraging sermon:

> *More and more people, indeed, are realising that the strenuous and unsettling times in which we live can be combated largely by some quiet and soothing effort with our hands and brain. All can be taken up with enthusiasm and often at little cost, and endless relaxation and enjoyment obtained.*

There were detailed plans for everything from a pencil case to *HMS Bounty*. In particular, there were plans for handy items like a handy coal box, a handy scissors sharpener, a handy tool carrier, a handy family savings box. There was a series of handy hints like when shoelaces become frayed to put a little glue on the end and twist them up. When they were dry they were as good as the metal tags any day. Another was a more efficient and quicker way to clean coins than using vinegar. The knack here was to rub them well with a damp cloth, on which was sprinkled some cleaning powder such as Vim. This quickly made them shiny and clean. There was a series on how to overcome, prevent and remedy some common camping troubles; how to solve candle-lighting trouble by placing the candle inside a glass jam jar on a windy night, or how to make a toothbrush out of a short length of wood, four inches in diameter, by cutting and re-cutting the end for a short distance in and softening it in water. The softened end cleaned the teeth well and should be held as a lady held her lipstick. The most fascinating section of all was the advertisements:

Blushing, shyness, nerves, self-consciousness, fears, ended.
Be taller. Quickly! Safely! Privately! No appliances, no tablets, no dieting.

I was really annoyed when I thought about *Hobbies Weekly* and compared it to the crap I had exchanged the swan's egg for. I had all the comics finished by Sunday night and was really cheesed off. I was lying in bed thinking what a fool I was: you could get comics anywhere, but where would I get another swan's egg? 'I might as well have a lash at writing a letter to *The Beezer* anyway,' says I, 'and see if I can recoup some of my losses.' So I got up and wrote them a letter telling all about our club hut in the quarry and the gang and our pastimes. I left out the bits about pilfering, and dolled it all up a bit to make it more respectable. I posted the letter on Monday and traded the load of stuff Waddler pawned off on me to an eejit from Old Youghal Road for a whole year's supply of *The Eagle*. I didn't feel too bad then.

The Eagle was well worth it. Some of it was as good as *Hobbies Weekly*. It had detailed cut-away plans of fascinating machines with an extensive list of their constituent parts: the *Lotus Formula I Grand Prix Car;* the *Baroudeur SE500 — a French Experimental Aircraft;* the *Dreadnought —* Britain's first Atomic Submarine; the *Rotterdam —* a 38,645 ton liner. It had a hobbies corner which featured playing cards, building your own library, making your own book-rack, model railways and how to build your own army. There were also four brilliant serials: a western, *Riders of the Range;* one on land, *Luck of the Legion;* one on sea, *Storm Nelson;* and one on space, *Dan Dare.*

When I came on the scene *Riders of the Range* was well advanced. Jeff Arnold, seriously wounded in his fight with Sam Bass — the bandit leader whom he taught to shoot —

has now recovered, but the doctor tells him that his right arm won't be properly healed for several months. In spite of this news, Jeff asks the Marshal of Dodge City to swear him in as deputy, so that he can go after Sam Bass and bring the bandit to justice. Jeff buys a Colt .35, which takes a much lighter load than a .45, and in less than a month can shoot left-handed. On the prairie wastes of Kansas, Sam Bass sneaks up on Jeff and says 'All right, old-timer, reach for the sky, or you're a dead man.' He laughs when he sees Jeff's right hand heavily bandaged and in a sling. Jeff replies, 'Howdy, I've got a little score to settle with you' and with a single left-handed shot, blows the gun clean out of Sam's hand. Moral of the story: the triumph of good over evil.

I just had to turn the page and I was in Indo-China with Sergeant Tough Luck, Corporal Trenet and Legionnaire Bimbery on the trail of Lord Tiger, a notorious bandit leader. When the CO of Post X ignores Luck's warning of an imminent attack by the bandits, the Legionnaires penetrate the jungle and find a treasure house full of ivory. Unfortunately Lord Tiger's thugs have got there first, so the three friends are forced to pursue and capture them before the bandits can take the news back to their master. But the trio are outnumbered and forced to surrender to their enemies. Suddenly Luck shouts 'Á moi, la Légion! Á moi, la Légion' and the three of them all lash out together shouting, 'Vive la Légion! Vive la Légion!' Though heavily outnumbered, their courage sees them through. Moral: fortune favours the brave.

After the jungle we set to sea with Storm Nelson and company who have been asked by Lloyd's to trap a mysterious figure who is responsible for the sinking of small heavily insured craft. In Algiers, Storm (posing as a smuggler) is introduced to a smuggler named White, whose twin brother, nicknamed 'The White Shadow', is trying to drive him out of business. Storm transports a cargo to Malta for White and, while he is awaiting instructions, his boy assistant, Kerfuffle, is kidnapped by 'The White Shadow', who also steals Nelson's contraband cargo. Meanwhile, in the labyrinthine caves and passages underneath the city of Valletta, Kerfuffle plans his escape: 'I'll take a tip from Theseus! Ariadne gave him a ball of thread to help him out of the maze — I'll use my shirt'. Back on the jetty, Storm and White begin their search for him:

'I'll take the main street'.'

'And I'll take the back street'.

'An' ah'll find Kerfuffle afore ye!'

Kerfuffle emerges from a cave beneath the jetty and leads them to the stolen cargo. Moral: a little classical learning goes a long way.

Dan Dare in full colour I always kept as a special treat till last. In *Trip to Trouble* Dan and Digby leave the orbiting Galactic Galleon in the aero car *Anastesia* to search for one of his crew taken prisoner by the warring barbarians of the planet Gaz, billions of miles away from earth. Dan and Digby themselves are captured by inhabitants of neighbouring Zyl. In order to show their captors the benefits of mechanisation Dan and Digby construct a primitive wheelbarrow. Suddenly Dan notices a fair-haired prisoner among the goggling spectators, who has the appearance of having worn civilised clothes. The evil Grandax of Gaz, with his radar-range deaf aids and ultra-directional microphones, hears their plan of escape and commands: 'Telo um dak, edar! (Get them fast!)

'Now we'll show 'em,' says Dan. A brief but furious battle ensues and our heroes escape with their heli-kits strapped to their backs. Moral: there are more things in heaven and earth, Horatio, than are dreamt of in your philosophy.

For about a week I soared on wild flights of imagination on *The Eagle*'s back. I awoke knackered every morning having been all over the world, and even miles away in outer space. It wasn't easy to pretend I was doing home work stuck upstairs all evening and summer holidays approaching. After I began to fight and roar in tongues in my sleep my father confiscated the lot, and I think my mother was relieved when I was back on the streets as brash and bold and normal as ever again.

5

TRAVEL

The environs of the fisheries were so varied and challeng-
ing that we rarely felt the urge to travel east of Silver
Springs or west of the Coliseum cinema. But occasionally
our interest was aroused by outside influences and we got
the travel bug. When we were down 'The Haunted' one day
Waddler and myself could hear all the commotion across
the river near the Athletic Grounds. When I got home I
mentioned it at tea time and my father said 'twas the opening day of the Cork Agricultural Show.

We knew nothing about agriculture but the word 'show'
sounded promising, and next morning Waddler and myself
headed off up the road, across the river, and down the
Marina to search for adventure and witness this spectacle.
We miscalculated the distance. 'Twas one thing to hear the
craic across the river: 'twas another thing to walk the five
miles all around to get there. When we did eventually we
were knackered. To add insult to injury we were expected to
pay to get in. Waddler was fit to be tied, but I said that
there was no point in losing the head over it. We'd find a
way like we always did.

There was a sort of goods entrance as well where all the
trailers with horses and sheep and cows drove in. We
decided to chance it with the sheep and hitch a ride with
them. They were more frightened by our presence than we
were by theirs and one of the shaggers had his arse through
the railing as I hung on at the back and he shat all the way
down my leg. Once inside we were fierce disappointed.
'Twas all about farm animals and machinery and show
jumping. We were starving at this stage and had to do
something about it. The IAWS stand had a kind of self-

91

service area at the back for the big nobs. 'Twas closed shop to the likes of us. They spotted us coming a mile away and booted us out. We knew that there was eating and drinking in a pint of stout and tried to hobble one each at the Guinness stand, but got caught.

'Twas a case of third time lucky. The ICA stand had a mouth-watering display of prize-winning confectionery from all over Munster: irresistible breads and jams and scones and cakes. The gentle giant of a farmer's wife who guarded the stand smiled at us as we passed by and we decided to chance her. Waddler strolled back and chatted her up about all the lovely cakes. She was bored at the time because no one had come near her yet, and was delighted with Waddler's company. She gave him a scone and a glass of milk and, while the two of them chatted away as happy as Larry, I sneaked up behind and stole an apple tart. That prize-winning apple tart from Ballydehob kept us going.

All the rest of the crap was for culchies and we found nothing to interest us except a notice that the DARE DEVIL MOTOR CYCLE TEAM would be performing in the afternoon. But they never put it on. I put it down as punishment for stealing the apple tart, and the long boring walk all the way back home again was our penance. By the time we got to Brian Boru bridge we were shagged. 'Twas all we could do to drag ourselves as far as Thompson's Bakery where we ate the breadcrumbs off the floor and washed them down with a slug from the water can used to fill the bread vans' radiators. When we reached St Patrick's church at the start of the Lower Road, we felt we had passed through the golden gates, and in no time at all we were back in the bosom of the family.

Our next expedition out was the enforced school tour to Dublin. We went by train. The only *craic* we had on the outward journey was when crossing the bridge at Mallow.

Where We Sported and Played

We all threw a penny out the window into the Blackwater for luck. Only Waddler got it wrong: he had a penny and a half-crown in his hand and he threw in the half-crown by mistake. He was in an awful state, but we all boxed in and gave him a penny and he was grand again. We had to make the statutory visit to the Zoo and were bored stiff by a dry ould lecture:

> The Zoological Gardens lie on both sides of a small valley which holds an artificial lake, and the water and the surrounding lawns, flower beds and shrubs combine to give the animals a particularly attractive setting. The exhibits of giraffes, lions and rhinoceroses are especially effective. Some of the islands in the lake have pairs of monkeys on them, while others have been organised to provide nesting sites for birds. There is a very large collection of water fowl from all parts of the world, as well as birds from Ireland.

We were much more interested in watching the chimps chewing the sweets we gave them like old men chewing tobacco, or just sitting there, carefree, scratching their heads and balls and all. The only other unusual matter of interest to us was the enormous size of the elephant shite and the frantic antics of two camels mating. All in all we were very disappointed with the Zoo and felt 'twas never worth it coming all the way up from Cork just to see a load of wild animals locked up in cages.

We weren't too impressed with O'Connell Street either. 'Twas too big and dirty, not like our own 'Pana' where you could cross at your ease. We were disgusted at the sight of Nelson still up there and decided that if we had the pillar in Cork we would have blown Nelson off it, and put Robert Emmet or Pádraig Pearse up instead. The trip to the Sláinte Mineral Water Co. Works made up for all the disappointment. We were fascinated by the thousands of revolving bottles as they jiggled along mechanically to be sterilised, filled, capped and labelled. The biggest thrill of all was at the end when we were given free drinks. Ricey was so excited that he got carried away, grabbed two bottles, and as he tilted his left hand, pouring one into his mouth, he automatically titled his right hand as well and poured the contents of the other bottle all down the side of his new overcoat.

We were all relaxed on the journey home and even Miss Byrne joined in the fun to break the monotony of the three and a half hour trip. She told us jokes from *The Bunty* like 'How high is a Chinaman?' and other ones about Paddy the Irishman, Paddy the Englishman and Paddy the Scotsman trying to get into heaven. Then one of the lads said he had one like that about the day Paddy the Irishman, Paddy the Englishman and Paddy the Scotsman met the devil, who agreed to let any of them who beat him in a game of catching go to heaven. Paddy the Englishman took off his shoe and threw it away up in the air, but the devil jumped up and caught it no bother. Paddy the Scotsman took a half-penny from his pocket and with all his might threw it away as far as he could but the devil flew off like a hawk and caught it. Then 'twas Paddy the Irishman's turn. He put his hands in his pockets, raised his right leg, left a mighty fart and said, 'Catch that!'

We were in stitches laughing at him. Miss Byrne was mortified, but realising that discretion was the better part of valour and that she would be wasting her time trying to put the boot in on the train anyway, said nothing. Our man became bolder and told another. 'What's the difference between a giraffe and a JCB? ... A JCB has a hydraulics'. This time we nearly shat ourselves in uncontrollable laughter, all the more boisterous because of Miss Byrne's presence. She got as red as a beetroot and got up and joined another group, more in embarrassment than in anger. To give her her due she had discreetly forgotten about it by the time we went back to school on Monday.

During the real summer months of June, July and August CIE ran special trains to Youghal on Sundays, and our mothers felt it part of their maternal obligation to expose their children to the seven miles of safe sandy beach and healthy salt water for the good of their health. We hated it. The hassle began at the unearthly hour of 9.00am on a Sunday morning. The squads of mothers and children that trickled in from Ballyphehane and down from Gurranebraher swelled to torrents by the time they reached the Lower Road, and we resented the intrusion of this mob on our otherwise orderly, peaceful surroundings. Snotty-nosed skinheads were running wild all over the platform, frightening the shite out of little babies in go-cars, who chewed ferociously on the dummies of empty sauce bottles. The gocars themselves were bedecked with enough equipment to keep an FCA contingent content for a week in camp: buckets and shovels, goggles and flippers, hurleys and sliotars.

Most important of all was the big net bag which contained the food and was guarded with as much diligence as if the Great Famine threatened again. To dare to open it before the appointed time would have been a major transgression. In any case hunger was a good sauce and the wait tended to add to the sense of expectation and belie the ordinariness of the contents: a dozen oranges and apples bought for 1s. 6d. up the Coal Quay on Friday; corned beef and banana sandwiches; two packets of Marietta biscuits; 6d. worth of mixtures or boiled sweets; and a big huge bottle of Cidona.

Of course such luxuries would not have been possible had we to pay for the train as well, and 'tis a great tribute to the humanity of railway porters and inspectors that we never did. The mothers angled the go-cars for the platform gate, switched into top gear authoritatively and, with a backward jerk of the head to the porter, said, 'himself is coming behind'. He's still coming. The excuse that we were given for his absence was that he was gone to a 'drag' or a 'bowl' or the Eucharistic Procession. To be fair to the more conscientious mothers they usually bought one ticket on which six people or more travelled.

On arrival, mother immediately handed out the swim suits and ordered us to strip. And because she insisted 'twas a grand day and that all this was good for us, we all pretended we were in the Mediterranean, that it was as warm over here as it was over there, and that those who wouldn't enter in were old yella bellies anyway. That feat of athleticism deserved its reward and we were given the Cidona and the Marietta, neither of which I since contemplate without seeing myself standing there, blue with the cold, my father's faded black togs dripping off me.

The highlight of the day was the evening tea. Mother made the long trek up Claycastle to the hamlet of bungalows to queue for boiling water. By the time she got back the tea was cold, had a bluish metal colour and was always too sweet. But, not to hurt mother's feelings after all her trouble, we drank it and ate the corned beef sandwiches, which by this time had a distinct taste of sand. Main course over we were given an orange and an apple — our weekly dose of vitamin C. These were all necessary, wholesome, obstacles on the way to the sweets, and we knew that our share of the same was contingent on our enthusiasm for the tea and sandwiches. They were worth the effort: acid drops, bulls' eyes and clove rocks; bits of Peggy's leg and gob-stoppers we crunched with such ferocity that we hardly knew whether 'twas the sweets or our teeth that we were swallowing.

About the time the Japanese began to market the transistor radio, Youghal was beginning to lose its attraction. You could listen to the Munster Final there on the strand but it wasn't exotic any longer. The Corporation killed it altogether when they began to include bathrooms in their new housing schemes in Fair Hill and Ballyphehane, and mothers didn't consider Youghal necessary any longer. But it left its mark on the generation of the 1950s and it still haunts me from Easter time on, when I can see my sister skipping in the lane, repeating the following nonsensical jingle:

> *We all went down to Youghal,*
> *We left the baby fall,*
> *Me mother came out*
> *And gave me a clout,*
> *And turned me into a bottle of stout.*

My parents decided that these Sunday trips to Youghal were not enough. So my father went into partnership with my uncle Denis and they bought an old 40 foot CIE coach, which my father converted into a holiday home. They located it in a Godforsaken spot at the other end of the beach in Youghal, five miles from anywhere, in a place called Redbarn. Even the barn had long since disappeared. It wouldn't have been too bad if it had been at the railway end, near Claycastle and the Merries. There were a lot of converted wagons and coaches here, even an old double-decker bus embedded in the soft green sward behind the sand dunes. 'Twas for all the world as if it had come on an excursion and got stuck here and they all said, 'arah, fuck it, let's chuck it', and left it there to rot. Only it didn't 'cause 'twas aluminium. Then someone with a big family came along and made a home of it, like the old woman who lived in a shoe.

Our coach was fairly primitive, but my father did a great conversion job. He sealed all the outer doors, except the one in the middle that served as our front door. He converted the compartment immediately inside it into a kitchen-cum-dining-cum-living-cum-sitting-room, containing such fixtures as a home-made dresser affixed to the wall, a long stool and an ingenious drop-leaf table hinged to the wall directly opposite the door. Two corridors led off the middle of this central area to two compartments containing bunks, and further, to the two end rooms on each side containing double beds. We were small and thought the place was huge. The only modern conveniences we had were a tiny electric stove, an electric kettle and a radio. On Sundays, the only day we saw other human beings in numbers, the radio was a great attraction, and crowds sat on the grass outside the kitchen window. My father turned the volume up full so that they could hear Mícheál Ó hEithir describe Tipperary or Kerry beating the shite out of Cork, depending on whether it was hurling or football.

A tiny lean-to contained a portable dry toilet for adult use only. We children felt this most unfair because we had to help my grandmother empty the contents into the sea at full tide in the middle of the night, and all we got for our trouble was the fascinating sight of the shimmering phosphorescence when the human waste hit the salt water.

Saturday afternoon was like Christmas, when a travelling shop in an old VW van with a broken exhaust arrived. We were allowed take our pick of the assorted sweets within a prescribed budget. I always went for fruit gums. You really got your money's worth for 3d. and the packet lasted for about two hours. On Sundays we had to walk all the way along the strand to mass. 'Twas dinner time when we got back again, shagged and starved. There was never any humming and hawing about the menu. Whatever was on we gobbled it all down in five minutes, even when 'twas pig's head and cabbage. On Sunday nights Alice and I often accompanied my grandmother to Clancy's bar. Somehow we didn't mind this journey and felt it was worth it. We were given a bottle of lemonade and grandmother drank two pint bottles of Murphy's stout. She was in her element then and, when her turn came around, would always sing 'The Stone Outside Dan Murphy's Door' and 'Kevin Barry'.

Where We Sported and Played

On the long walk home along the strand again she'd tell us stories to pass the time. She knew Cork like the back of her hand and told us all about the Cork arctic hero, Jerome Collins, a member of the ill-fated *Jeanette* expedition to the North Pole in 1879. His body was brought home from America in 1884. He was given a ceremonial funeral and the Bishop said: 'His body was brought home to his native city, mourned by two worlds, and nature herself shed a kindly tear upon his bier, while the storm-winds sang a parting requiem over his grave.' He's buried in the Curragh Kippane where a big Celtic Cross marks his grave.

She told us about all the famous Cork characters going back over the years like Harry Badger and Bothered Dan, former soldiers, who thought they were still fighting the Crimean war as they attacked and retreated up and down the North Main Street; Tom Green who had such a strange face that a foundry in the city offered him 5 shillings for a cast of it when they wanted something new in the line of hall-door knockers. But most of all she loved to tell of the heroic exploits of her famous ancestor, the great O'Sullivan Beare.

He was the last of the Irish patriots to hold out in Munster after the defeat at Kinsale in 1601 and, a year later at daybreak on 31 December 1602, set out from Glengarriff to march to Leitrim where O'Rourke, the Lord of Breifne, still held out. A big crowd of them set out, about twenty horsemen, four hundred soldiers and lots of women and children: about one thousand in all. A fortnight later only thirty-five of them reached O'Rourke's castle. The weather was shocking and they had to cross frozen mountains, snowed-up valleys and flooded rivers. To make matters worse they were attacked nearly every day by their enemies. On the first three days they were forced to travel eighty miles, had to fight two battles and hadn't time to set up camp and prepare a hot meal.

When they eventually got to the Shannon, the river

was in flood. No one was prepared to ferry them across, so they had to make their own boats. They cut long ash plants and arranged them in two rows opposite each other, their thick ends stuck in the ground and the other ends bent to meet each other opposite. They tied these together with ropes, and this formed the frame of the boat, turned upside down. Then they covered this skeleton with the skins of eleven horses and had a fine feed of horsemeat before heading off across the Shannon. But they weren't safe in Connacht either. They were attacked by a large force commanded by Malby at Aughrim. But no way was O'Sullivan Beare giving up now. They lashed into them and killed a hundred of the enemy, including Malby. O'Sullivan lost fourteen men but succeeded in routing the enemy and then hastening forward. The handful of them that eventually reached O'Rourke's castle in Leitrim had defied all the odds and won.

They kept the defiant spirit of freedom burning within the native Irish and served as a shining example of courage and determination to all of us, and in particular to those of the race of O'Sullivan Beare. Grandmother's mother was one of them and proud of it. She herself needed the same indomitable spirit to survive the tragedy in her own life. In her own way she passed it on to some of us grandchildren.

We had a barrel at the side of our coach to collect rain water for washing, but we had to forage for fresh water to make tea. 'Twas scarce and precious and some farmers none too willing to supply us from their wells. Sometimes we had to go considerable distances and to considerable efforts to acquire it. One day my father tried to carry two full buckets suspended from the handlebars of his bike but there wasn't too much left when he got back, so that was the end of that method. Then we raided from a nearby unfriendly well. He always took me with him as look-out and things were great for a week or so as we went off in the dead of night and were back in fifteen minutes with the goods.

Where We Sported and Played

Everything was grand until we got a bit cocky and blew it. One night my father hadn't secured the rope properly and, just as the bucket-full of water neared the brim of the well, the rope slipped and the lot went cascading 20 foot to the water below, clashing and clanging on its way. That was the end of that.

By this time things were beginning to look up in Redbarn and a row of chalets on the beach front, which the hobnobs from the city rented, shared a communal tap. Myself and John were getting buckets of water daily no bother, going the long way around and coming out from one of the gables so as they would all think we were in one of the chalets. That was grand for about a week until one day a brat from Christians stopped me and asked where I thought I was going with that bucket of water.

'Where d'ya think?' says I.

'I think you are stealing it,' he said.

'Well, if you want it you can have it,' says I, pouring it over him. With that his mother came around the corner. But she was a sound woman. She told him that 'twas his own fault for interfering, that water was cheap, that he should cop on to himself and that it would teach him a lesson to mind his own business in the future.

Rain or sunshine it didn't matter to my grandmother. If we were hanging around the door after breakfast she'd say 'get down dat strand ou' dat and don't be annoyin' your mother. There's plenty room for ye to play down there'. We played statues and buried each other in the sand in turn, played King Canute trying to hold back the tide and St Martin trying to put the sea into a hole. When we were in good form we worked together digging huge moats, and when we got fed up we trampled on each others' castles. After all the Sunday visitors had gone, we gathered all the boxes and cartons we could find at the high water mark and played shop, using sea shells as currency.

On a mild misty morning in August I got to the shop first

and said that it was strictly no credit that day, so they all went off along the strand to collect buckets of money. There wasn't much doing in the shop and I was delighted when a stranger approached, asked what I had in stock and what price everything was. I said that actually he was very lucky, that I always got fresh stock in on Monday and that I had some nice penny lollies, sweets and biscuits. He was dressed like a priest and I asked, 'Are you a priest?'

'No,' he said, 'a minister'.

'Oh,' I said, as if to say 'sorry, I shouldn't have asked that one', and added, 'it doesn't really matter anyway, 'cause you're a nice man.'

He looked disappointed all the same. He asked me if I knew my catechism and I said, 'Of course I do.'

Then he asked, 'Who made the world?' and I answered, 'God made the world'.

He continued, 'Who is God?' and I replied, 'God is our Father in Heaven, the Creator and Lord of all things.'

'Good boy,' he said, 'you know your catechism well. Now then, do you know the answer to this difficult one: why is the Catholic Church the one true church?' Had I stopped for a moment to think I might have pretended I didn't know, so as not to hurt his feelings. But I didn't and reamed off: 'the Catholic Church is the one true church because it was founded by Christ when he said to Peter: "Upon this rock I shall build my church and give to thee the keys of the kingdom of heaven. Feed my lambs, feed my sheep".'

He just gave a sad little smile and said nothing for a while. Then he asked if I had any ice-cream and I said, 'No, sorry, all sold out,' because I was embarrassed for hurting him and wanted him to go away. But we warmed to the game again and he promised to come tomorrow and bring real ice-cream and help me sell it for real money to the crowds that would come to buy from us. And I said, 'Great! Yipee!' But he never came and when I thought about it afterwards I prayed that my Catholic triumphalism didn't upset his meditations too much as he walked along the deserted strand.

When we came back from Redbarn at the end of August 1964 I was famous. The letter I wrote to *The Beezer* after I blew the swan's egg had won the star prize.

I am writing to tell you about the club which two of my friends and I founded about six months ago. It all happened when my father was throwing out a lot of wood, and we decided to build a club hut with it. We started our own museum by collecting birds' eggs, sea shells, foreign coins, butterflies and horse brasses. We also have a good collection of comics. We each pay a weekly subscription of one shilling We have already saved £3 and are going to buy some indoor games with it. The club is progressing well and we are making various improvements.

An Electric Speedboat and a 10s. Postal Order to Timothy Delaney, 5 Rock Vale Tce., Lower Rd., Cork, Éire.

My father was thrilled and took me across to the river to test the speedboat. I could have gone by myself but I think he wanted to be seen with his now famous son. A big crowd gathered to watch us and they were all more interested in me than in the boat.

Shortly afterwards I got a letter from a fella in Ghana promising to send me a monkey suit if I'd send him the speedboat. I wasn't interested in a monkey suit but was sorry afterwards that I didn't send him the speedboat. I knew from school that the black babies were going through a tough time just then, the same as we did during the Great Famine, and there was some Irish missionary out there in the bush awfully disappointed and embarrassed when I didn't deliver, after he telling all of them how kind and generous the Irish were. I vowed to St Anthony that I'd make it up to the black babies some day and so, sure enough, four years later he providentially gave me an opportunity to do so.

CONFESSION

We were well schooled in the theoretical side of confession. We knew all about states of grace, venial sin, mortal sin, committed with full knowledge and full consent, the rewards of heaven for the just *which no eye hath seen nor ear heard*, and the everlasting damnation of hell for the wicked *where there shall be weeping and gnashing of teeth*. A series of horror stories had brought it home to us that, tempting and all as a temporal fling would be, 'twould be foolish to blow the bliss of heaven, where we would be strolling around in beautiful pleasant surroundings eating chocolate for all eternity, for a few Toblerones or Woodbines here on earth below. We should remember that devils crowd around us, like the monk on his death-bed, to prevent us going to confession. We should remember that we would pay for our neglect like the sister of St Damien who went to purgatory for eighteen days because she listened to a song instead of going to confession; even worse still the dead nun who appears to her sister and says she is damned for having concealed a sin in confession; and worst of all the woman who, having concealed a great sin in confession, goes home and hangs herself.

To give Pádraig Ó Duinnín his due he often tried to temper the horror with some light anecdotes like the one about the cute Cavan traveller who went to confession and skipped merrily through his standard list of sins: 'forgot to say my morning and night prayers, father; took the Holy Name in vain and cursed the cow when she kicked the bucket; listened to a lot of idle talk about my neighbours, father; and I stole a bit of rope, father.'

'Was it a good bit of rope?' the priest asked.

'Only an old bit of *súgán*, father.'

'Sure that's no sin at all.'

'Ah, but don't you see, father, 'twas like this: there was a horse tied to the rope.'

The comic relief was only temporary for a grievous sinner like me and I often thought that when faced with a choice between the hassle of the confessional inquisition or the fire and brimstone of hell, I'd take my punishment like a man and choose the latter. I was faced with just such a dilemma after the job we did on the boat club. We were so professional in removing the lead piping that was used to supply the gas heaters years previously that nobody ever missed it. Being so easy made it too good to be true, and I couldn't enjoy the 30 shillings we got for the load. We had moved up a gear as pilferers, no longer interested in the petty removal of discarded items from back gardens and out-houses. We were now into breaking and entering and stealing, and getting away scot free. In my heart and soul I knew that if we didn't pay for it in this life we surely would in the next.

I eventually decided that confession of the big boat club rip-off in my own parish church of St Patrick's was out of the question. This was a job for the professionals, the order men who specialised in big sinners and who went on special missions once a year fishing for souls like mine. I knew that *they* couldn't be shocked: they had seen and heard everything during their time on the foreign missions among the pagans everywhere from Soho to Shanghai. The lead weighed heavily on my conscience and, as I lay awake at night, I could sometimes hear the gentle invitation, come to me all of you who are burdened and I will give you rest, and at other times the not so gentle warning, repent and be reconciled for you know not the day nor the hour when the Lord will come like a thief in the night.

Finally, when I felt I could postpone the day of reckoning no longer, I set to sizing up my chances with the order men. For starters the choice was reduced to three, on the grounds of familiarity: the Augustinians, the Dominicans and the Capuchins. The former ruled themselves out on the grounds of austerity. My sins were only more thorns in the crown on Christ's head in the Crucifixion scene in their Washington Street HQ. The Capuchins we met once a year on the feast of St Blaise when we went to have our throats blessed by them on Morrison's Island. I always thought they looked a bit weird with their skull caps like wooden soup bowls, long straggly beards, bare feet and long brown habits that made them the very picture of death. That only left the Doms. I knew nothing about them except that St Thomas Aquinas, the patron saint of scholars, was one of them, and I loved the plain chant of the hymn *Veni Creator* which we learned for mass on his feast day. I convinced myself as well that the Doms, in their flowing white habits, were as caring and kind and gentle as nurses.

On that Saturday evening St Mary's Pope's Quay was immaculate, smelling of polish and incense, and alive with the soothing hum of a pious procession of devotees doing the stations. Outside each confessional a red light indicated whether or not the priest was doing business. On home ground in St Patrick's one could judge a confessor's leniency or otherwise by his popularity. Here there was no such indicator, with an even scattering of earnest penitents outside each confessional. I looked at the names and eventually decided to chance one because the name sounded soft and familiar.

'Bless me, father, for I have sinned. 'Tis a month since me last confession, father.'

'Isn't that an awful long time for a young fellow like you?'

''Tis, father.'

I knew then that I was in trouble. This guy was on the ball and all into the Sergeant Major stuff I was trying so much to avoid.

'Be more regular in future. Now tell me, my child.'

Already he had unnerved me a bit and upset my carefully-laid strategy of shooting through my list, placing the grievous sins in such a way that the venials would cushion and take the monstrous look off them. As it happened I finished with the clanger.

'Forgot to say my morning and night prayers, father; took the Lord's name in vain; was cursing, father; was disobedient at home and at school, father; bullied my brother and stole a bit of lead, father.'

'Stole what?'

'A bit of lead, father.'

'How much lead did you steal?'

'A good bit, father.'

'How much did you get for it?'

'30 shillings, father.'

'You will have to make restitution.'

'Can't, father. We spent the money.'

'May God in his mercy forgive you. Anything else?'

'I lassoed a swan, father.'

'What!'

'A swan, father. I lassoed her to drag her off the nest to get the eggs.'

'Oh my God! Cruelty to one of His creatures and stealing and kidnapping her young. That is disgraceful conduct for a boy of your age. Now, is there anything else?'

I was as near to wiping the slate clean now as I ever was, and I reckoned he was as mad as he was going to be. So I decided to sock the last one to him quickly and have done with it.

'I stole some badges, father.'

'What do you mean you stole some badges?'

'The badges that do be on different makes of cars, father.'

'What badges?'

'A jaguar on a Jaguar, a big eagle on a plaque from a

108

Bedford lorry, a tiny little coloured shield with a castle in the middle from a Volkswagen, and a roundy metal thing with three silver stars stuck in shiny red plastic from a Ford Anglia.'

'You're a right little thief!' and he spat the 'th' at me. 'The likes of you should be locked up. You're a disgrace to your family and a menace to society. Say the fifteen decades of the Rosary for your penance and ask God earnestly to grant you forgiveness. I confess...'

In my confusion and shame I got stuck half-way through the Confetior and launched into the Memorare. It seemed more appropriate, given that he was a raging lion ready to devour me: 'Remember O most gracious Virgin Mary, that never was it known that anyone who sought thy aid or fled to thy protection was left unaided...'

He was finished the *Absolvo* before I was through and I heard him mumble to himself 'O my God, my God!' at my confused prayer. I could sense him becoming more and more impatient, and my voice trailed off in fear when I got to 'inspired with this confidence...'

'Go home and learn your prayers,' he said, dismissing me.

I left the box shell-shocked and indignant. I had been sure that an experienced Dom would have before now known some of the joy of heaven at the penitence of one great sinner rather than of the ninety-nine just who need it not, and that he would have been happy to land another big fish like me. I knew the Lord himself was much more sympathetic to my position and, anyway, the lead was no use to anyone, one of the eggs was a *gliogar*, and I was heartily sorry if I scraped any of the cars when I was prising off their badges with a six-inch nail. That was the end of the Doms as far as I was concerned, and you'd never find me inside one of their confession boxes again. I'd stick to my own diocesan crowd from now on, and be guided by the principle that the devil you know is better than the devil you don't.

In preparation for First Communion only one of the ten commandments was really stressed: the fourth (honour thy father and thy mother). By the time Confirmation came around the stress lay heavily on the sixth and ninth, and their derivatives: thou shalt not commit adultery; thou shalt not covet thy neighbour's wife. We knew all the theory about lust being one of the seven deadly sins, the importance of reciting three Hail Marys for purity every day, and had the heroic picture of Maria Goretti before us — she died before she'd commit sin. All of this was meant to make us scrupulous, and eventually it did, but our initial reaction to this emphasis on purity was one of curiosity. Eventually we put two and two together and realised that there was some relationship after all between this emphasis in school and some of our recent experiences in the world outside.

On our round selling sticks on a Saturday recently Waddler and myself called to the flats and your wan downstairs said come in when we knocked. We were flabbergasted when we beheld facing us, like the guns of Navarone, the finest pair of knockers you ever saw. We gazed in inquisitive stupefaction, and when she realised that we got a bigger thrill than she did, she threw us out. Afterwards we figured she must have been expecting someone else.

About a week after that another girl teased us when we called. Her mother was at work and she deliberately leaned out low over the window sill and shifted giddily from elbow to elbow, delighting at our excitement as we focused on her cleavage. We knew she was a right ould fla and it felt great that we were big enough now for her to be interested in us. She really got us going when she said that she'd leave us in for a quick flash if we wanted. We gasped with excitement, but there was a snag: she'd only leave us in one by one and we'd have to flash as well. But we funked it because, for all our bravado, we were scared and didn't have a clue. We couldn't make up our minds afterwards whether we were happy or sorry that we didn't take a chance.

When we opened our eyes and took a good look around we could see that they were all at it. There was a pop song in the charts at the time called 'Multiplication' and that song seemed to have something to do with the sexual fever that gripped us. 'Twas everywhere. One of the lads saw his sister and her boyfriend messing, she nibbling his left ear while he groped at her left breast. On the way from the shop another night the two of us saw a couple hurrying up Beale's Hill, a well-known nobbers' haunt: your wan was wriggling her chest enticingly and then running away, while your man ran after her in excited anticipation, rubbing his hands together and tipping her on the arse alternately.

Then all of a sudden one day in the quarry the bubble burst for us too. We got fed up of playing cowboys and Indians; our sisters got fed up of playing *tigh*, and we all paired off up the Black Hole. Like the first fag and drink, the first contact was revolting. In no way was lying there on the ground of a hard damp cave, nuzzling up against someone's cheek and you hardly able to breathe, as enjoyable as the games of winners and losers we knew. We were just about to give up and return to our happy childish pursuits when a girl who worked as an usherette in a cinema, and who was well experienced in these matters, came in and instructed us as to how to kiss on the lips and breathe and relax at the same time. Then she re-arranged the pairings and I was put with her sister who was twelve, the same age as myself.

Unlike me, she was no novice. She caressed with her tongue and wriggled and rubbed against my body. Everything was warm and soft and relaxed and comfortable. I felt a burning sensation in my groin as she took my

111

hand and began to rub it gently up and down her thigh then inside her dress, and my mind became a blissful muddle. I became carried away and lost track of time and place. By the time I came back to reality 'twas tea time and I was no longer a child. We all knew that 'twas the end of cowboys and Indians and *tigh*. Things would never be as blissfully ignorant or free any more and, like the survivors of a bomb blast, we all drifted off aimlessly and individually home for tea.

I felt lousy and couldn't eat. Food disgusted me. I felt dirty and imagined sores breaking out all over my polluted flesh. I had entered the adult world of sin and it haunted me morning, noon and night. I became insecure and suspicious, morose and surly. This went on for five weeks and I knew that mother began to notice. She said nothing but I could see that she was keeping a close eye on me. When Lent came around I determined to make a serious effort to get back on the straight and narrow again. Night after night I prayed for the grace and courage to make a good confession, but after my experience with the Doms two years previously, courage was not forthcoming. But God works in mysterious ways and quite by accident He gave me a break towards the end of Lent.

'Twas a Thursday night and I had gone up to Mayfield to do a comic swap with Tim Cantillon. When we had our business finished and both of us happy he said he'd accompany me as far as the new church to go to confession for the first Friday on the morrow. He said that they had a new young priest who was a cinch and that I should try him. I had read a whole lot of stories about divine intervention and all that road to Damascus kind of stuff. I looked down and thought for a minute. I imagined things should have been a bit more dramatic, with the beautifully-lit new church on the top of the hill on one side, and on the other the darkness of the way I had come from the Lower Road. I pictured God and the devil fighting

for my soul where I stood, and Cantillon swung it for God:
'sur' you might as well go to confession too, and when you go
home your mother will be delighted and she'll leave you
up again next week.'

Whatever about this new young priest being as nice as
Cantillon said, I knew he couldn't be as bad as the Domin-
ican lion so I took the plunge. 'Bless me, father, for I have
sinned. 'Tis seven weeks since me last confession, father.'

I skipped all the gimmicks and tactics this time and
jumped straight in: 'I put my hand up a girl's dress, father.'

'Why did you do that, my child?'

'Because she wanted me to, father.'

His tone was gentle and understanding. I felt my
courage and honesty were being rewarded and that he was
on my side. He was here to lead me from the darkness of sin
into the light of grace. He continued sympathetically: 'And
what age are you?'

'Twelve, father.'

'And what age was the girl?'

'Twelve too, father.'

'And where did all this happen?'

'Ye see we were playing nobbers up the Black Hole,
father.'

'What were you playing?'

'Nobbers, father. Ye know, kissin' and all that kind of
stuff that the grown-ups do be doing.'

'I see. And did you ever learn about the sins of the flesh
in school?'

'Oh yes, father. We did everything about pride,
covetousness, lust, anger, gluttony, envy and sloth. We were
told to say three Hail Marys for purity every night and to
repeat after each of them 'O Mary conceived without sin,
pray for us who have recourse to thee'.

'And do you say those prayers every night?'

'I always do for the first few days after confession,
father, then I forget.'

113

Where We Sported and Played

'Do your best to remember in future and they will help you to avoid occasions of sin.'

'Yes, father.'

'Now is there anything else on your mind?'

'There is, father. I committed sacrilege, father.'

'Well, you had better tell me about it.'

'You see, father, the last time I went to confession I got excited and frightened when the priest started giving out to me, and I left out the sin I'm just after telling you a minute ago.'

'And were you truly sorry for your sins the last time?'

'Oh, I was, father.'

'And are you truly sorry now for not having the courage to confess all your sins the last time?'

'Indeed I am truly sorry, father.'

'Then God will forgive you, my son. I confess...'

I never made an act of contrition before or after with such earnestness. Tears of joy at my salvation swelled up in my eyes; I bowed my head and asked for God's mercy and beat my breast saying I was heartily sorry for having offended. In the silence that followed our prayer all was celestial serenity and peace.

I came out of the box and felt that I could almost fly. Pádraig Ó Duinnín's exhortations were right after all: God never closed one door but he opened another; seek and you will find. 'Come to me all of you who are burdened and in labour and I will give you rest, for my yoke is easy and my burden light.' I slept real well that night and could see the relief on mother's face the next morning when she recognised that I was back to my old self again.

The old self, however, was no longer a child. I had tasted good and evil and was now a young man at the crossroads. My carefree childhood, where the world hardly existed beyond the extremities of the Lower Road, was over. The world beckoned. My parents believed that education sets you free, and had come to the firm conclusion that school was more important than boxing. By sheer chance someone else in the railway had a son doing the entrance examination for Farranferris, the junior seminary for the diocese of Cork and Ross, and father got the idea that a dramatic change like this was needed to keep me out of devilment. Given my achievements in national school, *The Beezer* and all, he was convinced that the exam would be no problem to me.

I was a nervous wreck for days before the test, torn between the temptation to make a hames of it and satisfy my own wish to go to Crawford Tec. and qualify as an electrician, or play out of my skin and take a quantum leap up the social ladder to fulfil my parents' aspiration for me. I couldn't decide between them, but in the end the latter choice, for once, came naturally to me. For the life of me I could never figure out why, for I found Farranferris awesome even before there was any possibility that I'd end up there: a big sturdy red-bricked lump of a giant presbytery lording it over Blackpool from the brow of Spangle Hill, like a giant slumbering hippopotamus.

Though there in the heart of the city, it was run very much by West Cork for West Cork. Even getting there was like the ascent from the Inferno, through a maze of pokey decayed lanes off the Watercourse Road. It was enclosed by a huge wall of 9" x 4" solid blocks on the flat. There must have been at least two and a half million of them. A beech-lined avenue led from the gate to a series of peaceful and meditative walks radiating from the white statue of our Lady in the rock garden, and ending in two straight lines at Calvary and Bishop Murphy's grave. Inside the door all was monastic austerity: solid black and white tiled floor, pitch-pine woodwork and a strong smell of polish. A white marble bust of Bishop Delaney kept watch from the window-sill facing the door; a statue of the Blessed Virgin dominated the courtyard; the class halls were arranged in a rectangle all around with the College Chapel and Refectory as focal points directly opposite each other. Gothic scrolls adorned the entrances to both: *Ave Maria; Ora pro Nobis; Gloria in Excelsis Deo.* And the walls of the refectory were bedecked with the portraits of past presidents and bishops, serving as examples for our inspiration and edification.

This wasn't my scene at all: all this sanctified odour of ecclesiastical splendour was light years removed from the Dickensian ordinariness of Rock Vale, and I felt like a fish out of water. I had never seen so many religious together in one place before. Unlike the rest of the Farna aspirants I had no relations in the Church, except for mother's first cousin who joined a French order of nuns and was never heard of again. And I had never spoken to a priest man to man. When the curate called for his dues mother always gave him two half-crowns, and he always gave back one. He asked sternly if we, the children, went to school and said our prayers, but he never spoke to us.

Once when the mission was on and a Passionate was visiting an old lady on our lane he stopped and spoke to me. I was so surprised that I was tongue-tied and couldn't answer. At another time, having served early morning mass on a shocking morning during Lent, I was so amazed when Fr O'Riordan gave me a lift home that I couldn't find the door handle to open the door of his car. I thought that all religious belonged to a different world from us completely, that they didn't even go to the toilet. And the joke about the nun who caught two lads at school competing to see which of them could pee highest up the wall, when asked by the reverend mother what she did, replied 'Oh! I hit the roof!' was the most revolting I had ever heard.

So, like all the major things that happened in my life I did the entrance examination for Farna purely by chance, just because someone else in the railway had a son doing it. The exam part of it I didn't mind — the Irish, English and Maths — but the rest of the procedure was all serious, like a formal initiation ceremony. We were taken in charge for the day by senior prefects, right rocks of commonsense, the sons of wealthy West Cork farmers, in their corduroy trousers, check sports jackets with leather armpads and strong hardwearing leather shoes. They supervised us in groups of twelve and divided the food (soup and salad) among us in the refectory at lunchtime in a scrupulously fair way. They escorted us from one hall to another and introduced us to the grand inquisitor who interviewed each of us individually.

The Irish interview was grand, all artificial school stuff about the weather, nature and history, which you either knew or you didn't. But the English was murder. All I had was street English. When addressing my ecclesiastical superiors I had been instructed that a humble 'yes' or 'no', 'I do' or 'I do not, father' would suffice. When expected to talk man to man in a situation like this across the table I was lost. It must have been worse for Fr Lenihan, trying to draw some kind of coherent information out of me, to be able to get some idea of what kind of character I was. I reckon that in the end he must have given me some kind of sympathy vote.

Mother was in an awful quandary on Saturday morning when Fr Nagle called. He had been for his Easter dues a fortnight before so it was not the ritual visit. When he asked for me she turned pale, thinking the worst, like maybe I was the number one suspect for stripping the lead off the roof of the church. Then the truly miraculous happened: Fr Nagle smiled, offered his hand and said, 'Teddy, me boy,' as though he had known me all his life, 'put it there.' He explained that he had got a call from the President of Farranferris offering me a place. Mother clasped her hands, raised her eyes to heaven and said, in as much relief as gratitude, 'Thanks be to God'.

Just then father came in from work and, when he heard the news, insisted that he knew all along that I had what it takes, and that he knew that time would tell. And the more he pretended he wasn't surprised the more he couldn't contain himself. He rejoiced over me like the prodigal son returned home. By evening all the road knew that I had 'got the call' and might even be a priest. I began to believe that it was possible myself. After all, greater gurriers than me, like David and Paul in the Bible, had been called and turned to the Lord. Maybe some great vocation was in store for me too on the road through Farranferris, *ach sin scéal eile agus beidh lá eile chun a inste, le cúnamh Dé.*

GLOSSARY

Chapter 1.

Crap	Rubbish
Craic	Fun, amusement
Tripe and drisheen	Cork dish/the lining of sheep's stomach and pig's gut.
Crúibíns	Pig's feet
Shillelagh	Blackthorn cudgel
Fal-doll	Gaudy ornament
Raza	Raspberry cordial
A few bob	Bob = one shilling in old currency.

Chapter 2

Goner	Finished
Skidaddle	Make a quick get away
Bulling	Boasting, telling tall tales
The soot of it	The satisfaction of it
Knackered	In big trouble
Scew-ways	Awry
Béal bocht	Poor mouth
Hobble	Steal
All a ba	A sort of 'free for all' way of distributing goodies
Slogs	Slaps across open palm with stick or leather.
Big shot	Hero
Jumped up	Sophisticated
On the lang	Mitching/truant from school without parents' permission
Padhsán	Weak, nervous person
Wopper	Big beauty
Gowl	Fool

Tocht	Lump in throat
A dead cert	Sure to succeed
Pep	Vigour
Savvy	Commonsense, understanding

Chapter 3

Plámás	Flattery
Tá	Yes
Seas	Stand
Suigh	Sit
Ciúnas	Silence
Feidhleachán	Butterfly
Sciathán dearg	Red wing
Sciathán buí	Yellow wing
Lick	Sycophant
Tuatha Dé Dannan	People forced underground by the invading Fir Bolg and who became fairies
Fir Bolg	Belly men (legendary invaders)
Leprechaun	Fairy folk of Ireland
Planked	Hidden
Maidrín-a-rua	Little red dog (fox)
Yobo	Yahoo
An bhfuil cead agam dul amach, más é do thoil é	May I go out, please (to the toilet)
Pot luck	Pure chance
Sliotar	Small hard cork, latex ball used in hurling
Modh díreach	Direct method
Aon rud eile anois?	Anything else now?
Ceart go leor	All right
Tanner	Six old pence
Came up trumps	Did not let you down, delivered the goods

Where We Sported and Played

On a roll	Hitting a purple patch
Saved my bacon	Got me out of a tight spot
Cinch	Simple task
Cake-walk	Simple (American:piece of cake)
Cigire	Inspector
Aon, dó, trí	One, two, three
Hardchaw	Tough guy
Céilí	Irish dance
Lasher	Beauty
Play by ear	Be attentive and respond promptly as the situation demands
Fallaí Luimní	Walls of Limerick
Ionsaí na hInse	Siege of Ennis
Cor Beirte	Two-hand reel
Daw	Idiot
Away on a hack	On to a winner
Baint an Fhéir	Haymaker's Jig
Amhrán na bhFiann	National Anthem
To give a fifty	Let somebody down, deliberately disappoint
Fear an tí	Master of ceremonies
Ach	But
An chéad leaba i lár baill sa seomra fada	The first bed in the centre row in the long room
An bhfuil tú cinnte gur tusa atá i gceist?	Are you sure that you are the person in question?

Chapter 4

Lost the rag	Flew into a temper
Starkers	Naked
Gawk	Stare or gape
Gallivanting	Roaming around
Mar dhea	Make believe

Where We Sported and Played

Bucking	Mad
Knacker	Scrap merchant
Flayed out	Very tired
Closest shave	Narrowest escape
Shriven	Absolved
Funking it	Chickening out, avoiding
A stone's throw	Short distance
Hobble	Steal
Gliogar	Empty egg
Knack	Trick
Have a lash	Have a go
Dolled up	Embellished
Knackered	Exhausted

Chapter 5

Fit to be tied	Speechless
Big nobs	Nobility
Culchies	Contemptous term for country people
Shagged	Exhausted
Boxed in	Contributed
Put the boot in	Get tough
Hassle	Bustle and trouble
Drag	Drag hunt with hounds
Bowl	Road bowling played along rural roads in Cork and Armagh
Yella bellies	Cowards
Clout	A clatter across the face
Humming and hawing	Vacillating

Chapter 6

Súgán	Straw rope
Clanger	The big one, mistake
Fla	An easy ride

Where We Sported and Played

Nobbers	Courting couples
Tigh	House
A hames	A mess
Pokey	Small, narrow
Ach sin scéal eile	But that's another story
Agus beidh lá eile	And there'll be another day
Chun a inste	To tell it
Le cúnamh Dé	With the help of God

LOVELY IS THE LEE

Robert Gibbings

Lovely is the Lee, a beautifully illustrated book with wonderful wood engravings, begins in Galway, far away from the source of the Lee. A tour around Connemara gives us some pleasant sketches of púcáns, donkey-carts and cottages; Cong brings us antiquities, flint arrow heads and the like. Next we find ourselves in Inisbofin and in Aran and then we find ourselves in Cork – which Robert Gibbings claims is the loveliest city in the world:

> Cork is the loveliest city in the world. Anyone who doesn't agree with me either was not born in the city or is prejudiced. The streets are wide, the quays are clean, the bridges are noble ... It is such a friendly city, too. People that you never met in your life stop you in the street ...

THE FARM BY LOUGH GUR

Mary Carbery

The Farm by Lough Gur is the true story of a family who lived on a farm by Lough Gur, the Enchanted Lake, in County Limerick. Their home, shut away from the turmoil of politics, secure from apprehension of unemployment and want, was a world in itself.

THE TAILOR AND ANSTY

Eric Cross

"'Tis a funny state of affairs when you think of it'. It is
the Tailor himself speaking. 'The book is nothing but
the fun and the talk and the laughter which has gone
on for years around this fireside ...'

The Tailor and Ansty was banned soon after its first publi-
cation in 1942 and was the subject of such bitter controversy
that it may well have influenced the later relaxation of
the censorship law. Certainly it has become a modern Irish
classic, promising to make immortals of the Tailor and his
irrepressible foil, his wife, Ansty, and securing a niche in
Irish letters for their Boswell, Eric Cross.

The Tailor never travelled further than Scotland, from
Gearnapeaka, near Gougane Barra, and yet the width of
the world can hardly contain his wealth of humour and
fantasy.

STORIES FROM THE TAILOR

edited and translated by
Aindrias ó Muimhneacháin

The Tailor was a remarkable storyteller and he has his
own special way of telling stories. Aindrias Ó Muimh-
neacháin has edited and translated these wonderful stories
and they are now available for the first time in English.
We see the Tailor's humour and laughter and his extra-
ordinary spirit shines through all his stories.

MY NEW CURATE
Canon P. A. Sheehan

'It is all my own fault. I was too free with my tongue. I said in a moment of bitterness: "what can a Bishop do with a parish priest? He's independent of him." It was not grammatical and it was not respectful. But the bad grammer and the impertinence were carried to his Lordship, and he answered: "What can I do? I can send him a curate who will break his heart in six weeks ..."'

My New Curate is one of the most powerful of Canon Sheehan's very popular books. It was acclaimed all over the world as a vivid picture of the relationship between a priest and his flock and has now been reprinted for the benefit of whole generations who did not have the opportunity to read it.

AROUND THE BOREE LOG
and other verses

John O'Brien

Around the Boree Log is verse that is simple and sincere and lit with a kindly understanding of the lives it chronicles. In his affectionate and gently humorous verses John O'Brien sang of farming life and of the life of Irish settlers in Australia – at home, on the land, and at the Church upon the hill that is the centre of their lives.

Includes John O'Brien's best loved verses including 'The Little Irish Mother', 'The Trimmin's of the Rosary', 'The Altar Boy', 'Laughing Mary' and 'The Parting Rosary'.

ISLANDERS

Peadar O'Donnell

First published in 1927, this powerful novel depicts the life of a small island community in Donegal. It is a story of epic simplicity, of people who confront in their daily lives, hunger, poverty and death by drowings.

'*Islanders* would be worth reading merely as a description of the lives of the poor on a wild barren and beautiful coast, on which two bucketfuls of winkles may be a considerable addition to the wealth of the home. It is also a piece of heroic literature ...' *(Introduction by Robert Lynd)*

WEST BELFAST

Danny Morrison

'All over Belfast the blistering Sunday afternoon sun drew young and old alike outdoors.

'Some people had small front gardens in which to sit and relax. Others had gardens, back and front. But most working-class people, apart from those who had moved out to the new Housing Trust estates, sat at the doors of their brown terrace houses or in their backyards to be sunned ...'

West Belfast opens in an innocent setting of youthfulness. But as the children mature they do so against a dangerous background.

Danny Morrison creates the scene, paints beautiful word pictures and tells a fascinating story of love and tragedy set in the streets of war-torn Belfast.

ANNIE M.P. SMITHSON

The Walk of a Queen

Paid in Full

The Marriage of Nurse Harding

Her Irish Heritage

Nora Connor

Annie M.P. Smithson was the most successful of all Irish romantic novelists and all of her books were bestsellers:

THE WALK OF A QUEEN is a fascinating story of passion and intrigue set against a backdrop of the War of Independence.

PAID IN FULL is a story of love and courage.

THE MARRIAGE OF NURSE HARDING is a story of love, bigotry and heroism.

HER IRISH HERITAGE is another exciting love story.

NORA CONNOR is a fascinating romance of yesterday.